I0755447

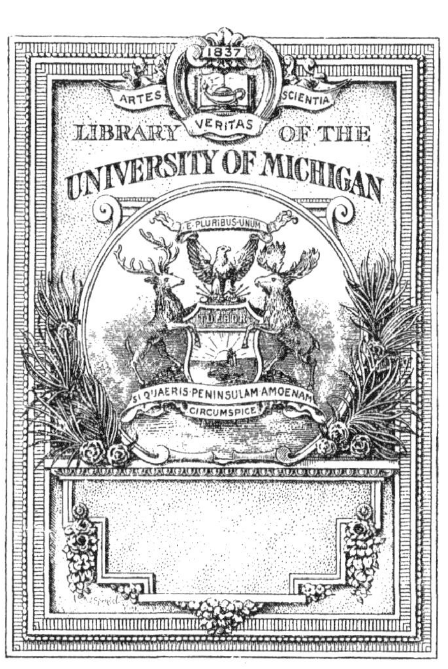
1837
ARTES
VERITAS
SCIENTIA
LIBRARY OF THE
UNIVERSITY OF MICHIGAN
E PLURIBUS UNUM
TUEBOR
SI QUAERIS PENINSULAM AMOENAM
CIRCUMSPICE

APPLETONS' POPULAR LIBRARY

OF THE BEST AUTHORS.

A JOURNEY TO KATMANDU.

MAP OF NEPAUL.

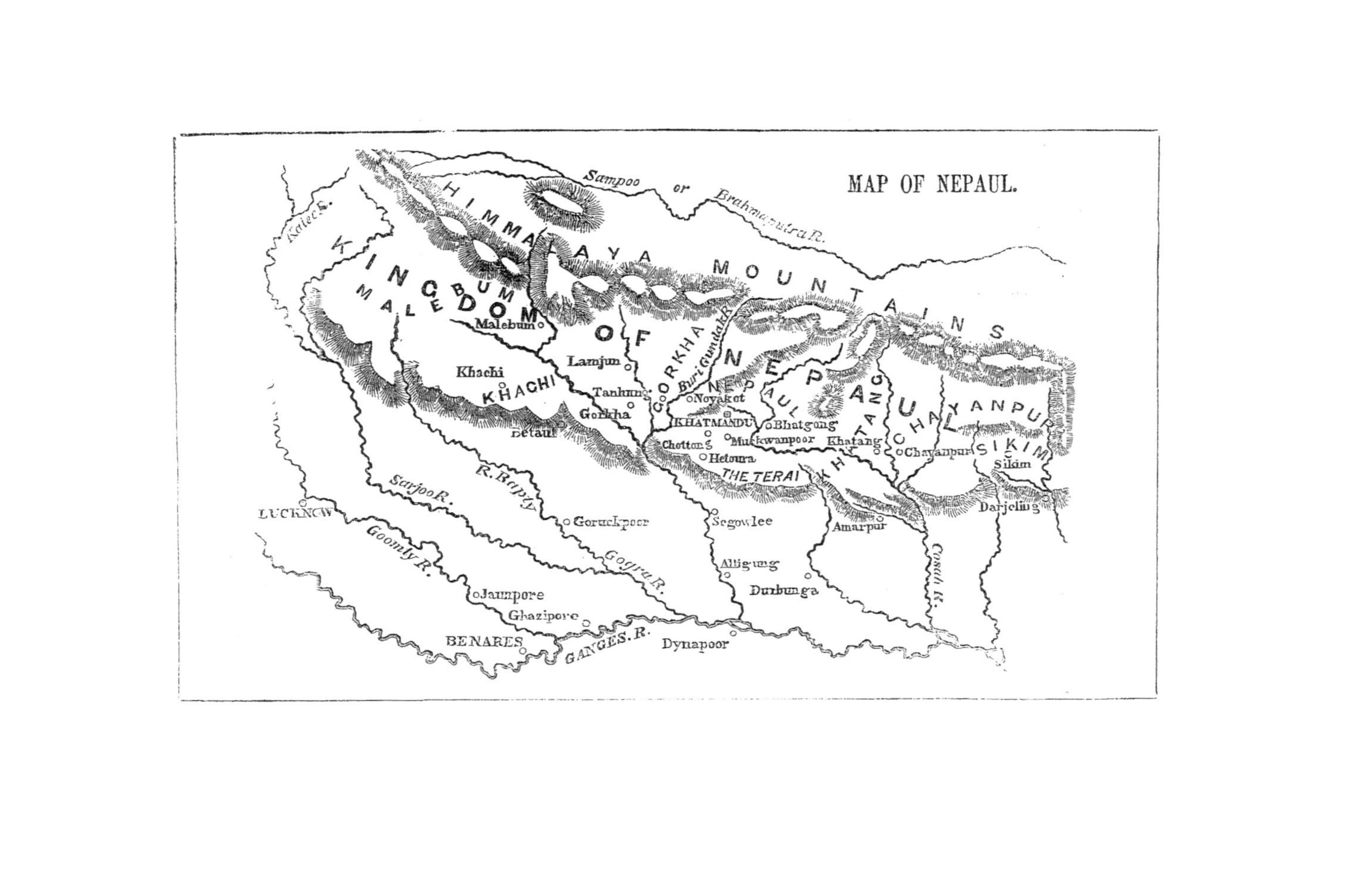

A

JOURNEY TO KATMANDU

(THE CAPITAL OF NEPAUL),

WITH

THE CAMP OF JUNG BAHADOOR;

INCLUDING

A SKETCH OF THE NEPAULESE AMBASSADOR AT HOME.

BY LAURENCE OLIPHANT.

NEW-YORK:
D. APPLETON & COMPANY, 200 BROADWAY.
M.DCCC.LII.

TO

SIR ANTHONY OLIPHANT, C.,B.,

CHIEF JUSTICE OF CEYLON,

THE FOLLOWING PAGES ARE INSCRIBED BY

HIS AFFECTIONATE SON,

THE AUTHOR.

PREFACE.

The interest which was manifested in the Nepaulese Embassy during the short residence of Jung Bahadoor in England leads me to hope that a description of the romantic country and independent Court which he came to represent, as well as some account of his own previous eventful career, may not be unacceptable to the English Public—more especially as no work upon Nepaul has been published in this country, that I am aware of, since Dr. Hamilton's, which appeared about the year 1819.

Through the kindness and friendship of the Nepaulese Ambassador, I was enabled to visit Katmandu under most favourable circumstances; and during the journey thither in his company I had abundant opportunity of obtaining much interesting information, and of gaining an insight into the character of the people, and their mode of every-day life, for which a residence in camp was peculiarly favourable.

In the Terai I was fortunate enough to witness the Nepaulese mode of elephant-catching, so totally unlike that of any other country, while the grand scale on which our hunting party was organised was equally novel.

I therefore venture to submit this volume to the public, in the hope that the novelty of a portion of the matter contained in it will in some degree compensate for its manifold defects.

CONTENTS.

CHAPTER I.

CHAPTER II.

CHAPTER III.

CHAPTER IV.

CHAPTER V.

CHAPTER VI.

CHAPTER VII.

CHAPTER VIII.

CHAPTER IX.

CHAPTER X.

CHAPTER XI.

CHAPTER XII.

CHAPTER XIII.

CHAPTER XIV.

CHAPTER XV.

CHAPTER XVI.

CHAPTER XVII.

CHAPTER XVIII.

A

JOURNEY TO KATMANDU,

&c. &c.

CHAPTER I.

Arrival of Jung Bahadoor in Ceylon—Voyage to Calcutta—Rifle practice on board the Atalanta—Rifle-shooting—Colonel Dhere Shun Shere—A Journey along the Grand Trunk Road of Bengal—The experimental railway—The explosion at Benares.

TOWARDS the close of the year 1850 a considerable sensation was created in the usually quiet town of Colombo by the arrival in Ceylon of His Excellency General Jung Bahadoor, the Nepaulese Ambassador, on his return to Nepaul, bearing the letter of the Queen of England to the Rajah of that country.

The accounts which had preceded him of the magnificence of the jewels with which his person was generally adorned, had raised expectations amongst the natives which were doomed to disappointment: intelligence had been received by Jung of the death of the Queen of Nepaul, and the whole Embassy was in deep mourning, so that their appearance on landing created no little astonishment, clad, as they all were, in spotless white, excepting their shoes, which were of black cloth—leather not being allowed to form part of the Nepaulese mourning costume.

His Excellency had a careworn expression of countenance, which might have been caused either by the dissipation attendant upon the gaieties of his visit to London, by grief for his deceased Queen, or by sea-sickness during his recent stormy passage across the Gulf of Manaar. He had been visiting sundry Hindoo shrines, and it was for the purpose of worshipping at the temple of Ramiseram, which is situate on the island of that name, in the Gulf of Manaar, forming part of Adam's Bridge, that he touched at Colombo. Here I was fortunate enough to make his acquaintance, and, attracted by his glowing description of sport in Nepaul, accepted an invitation to accompany him to that country, in order to judge of it for myself.

So good an opportunity is indeed rarely afforded to a European of visiting Nepaul, and of inspecting the internal economy of its semi-barbarous Court. I soon found that Jung Bahadoor excelled no less as a travelling companion than he had done as Premier and Ambassador.

As doubts had arisen and some misapprehension had prevailed in England as to his position in his own country, I was anxious to ascertain what was his real rank and how he would be received there. It was reported that he had risked his temporal welfare by quitting his country, while, in order that his eternal welfare should in no way be compromised by this bold and novel proceeding, he had obtained an express reservation to be made in his favor at Benares, overcoming, by means of considerable presents, the scruples of a rapacious and not very conscientious priesthood.

The ostensible object of the mission had reference, as far as I could learn, to a portion of the Terai (a district lying upon the northern frontier of British India) which formerly belonged to Nepaul, and which was annexed by the Indian Government after the war of 1815–16; but it is probable that other motives than any so purely patriotic actuated the Prime Minister. His observant and inquiring mind had long regarded the British power in India with wonder and admiration—sentiments almost unknown amongst the apathetic Orientals, who, for the most part, have become too much accustomed to the English to look upon them with the same feelings as are entertained towards them by the hardy and almost savage race inhabiting the wild valleys of the Himalayas.

But besides the wish to gratify his curiosity, there existed yet another incentive which induced him to undertake this expedition. The precarious nature of his high position in Nepaul urged on him the good policy, if not the necessity, of a visit to England, for he doubtless felt, and with good reason, that the native Durbar would be inclined to respect a man who had been honored with an interview with the Queen of so mighty a nation, and had had opportunities of securing the support of her government, should he ever be driven to seek its aid.

* * * * *

The Atalanta, one of the oldest steam frigates in the Indian navy, had been placed at the disposal of His Excellency, and, upon the evening of the 9th of December, 1850, was lying in the Colombo Roads, getting up her steam as speedily as possible, while I was uneasily perambulating the wooden jetty, which is all the little harbor can boast in the shape of a pier, endeavoring to induce some apathetic boatmen to row me over the bar, a pull of three miles, against a stiff breeze. It was bright moonlight, and the fire from the funnel of the old ship seemed rushing out more fast and furious in proportion as the boatmen became more drowsy and immovable; finally they protested that it was an unheard-of proceeding for anybody to wish to go on board ship on such a night at such an hour, and insinuated that all verbal or pecuniary persuasions would be alike unavailing. It is very evident that Colombo boatmen are a thriving community; still they seem a timid race, for upon my having recourse to threats containing fearful allusions, which there was not the remotest possibility of my being able to carry into execution, a wonderful revolution was effected in the feelings of the sleepers around me; they forthwith began to unwind themselves from the linen wrappers in which natives always swathe themselves at night like so many hydropathic patients, and, converting their recent sheets into turbans and waist-cloths, they got with many grumblings into a tub-like boat, just as the smoke from the steamer was becoming ominously black. Their eyes once open, the men went to work in good earnest, and an hour afterwards I had the satisfaction of walking the deck of the Atalanta, which was going at her utmost speed, some seven knots an hour.

In the morning we were off Point de Galle, and put in there for General Jung Bahadoor, who, with some of his suite, had made the journey thither by land.

All the world make voyages now-a-days; and nobody thinks of describing a voyage to India any more than he would an excursion on the Thames, unless he is shipwrecked, or the vessel he is in is burnt and he escapes in an open boat, or has some such exciting incident to relate. We were *unfortunate* in these respects, but in our passengers we found much to interest and amuse us; and as everything regarding the Nepâulese Ambassador is received with interest in England, a description of the proceedings of one day, as a sample of the ten we spent on board the "Atalanta," may not be altogether uninteresting.

Time never seemed to hang heavy on the hands of the Minister Sahib, for that was his more ordinary appellation; rifle practice was a daily occupation with him, and usually lasted two hours. Surrounded by those of his suite in whose peculiar department was the charge of the magnificent battery he had on board, he used to take up his station on the poop, and the crack of the rifle was almost invariably followed by an exclamation of delight from some of his attendants, as the bottle, bobbing far astern, was sunk for ever, or the three strung, one below the other, from the end of the fore-yard-arm, were shattered by three successive bullets in almost the same number of seconds. Pistol practice succeeded that of the rifle, and the ace of hearts at 15 paces was a mark he rarely missed.

Then the dogs were to be trained, and in a very peculiar manner; a kid was dragged along the deck before the noses of two handsome stag hounds, who, little suspecting that a huge hunting-whip was concealed in the folds of their master's dress, were unable to resist so tempting a victim and invariably made a rush upon it, a proceeding which brought down upon them the heavy thong of the Minister Sahib's whip in the most remorseless manner. That task accomplished to his satisfaction, and not being able to think of anything else wherewith to amuse himself, it would occur to him that his horse, having thrown out a splint from standing so long, ought to be physicked. He was accordingly made to swallow a quantity of raw brandy! It was useless to suggest any other mode of treatment, either of horse or dogs. The General laughed at my ignorance, and challenged me to a game of backgammon. Occasionally gymnastics or jumping were the order of the day, and he was so lithe and active that few could compete with him at either.

While smoking his evening pipe he used to talk with delight of his visit to Europe, looking back with regret on the gaieties of the English and French capitals, and recounting with admiration the wonders of civilization he had seen in those cities. He was loudest in his praise of England. This may have arisen from a wish to gratify his auditory, and it certainly had that effect. He had not thought it necessary, however, to perfect himself in the language of either country beyond a few of what he considered the more important phrases. His stock consisted chiefly of—How do you do?—Very well, thank you—Will you sit down?—You are very pretty—which pithy sentences he used to rattle out with great volubility, fortunately not making an indiscriminate use of them.

But my particular friend was the youngest of his two fat brothers, whose merits, alas! were unknown in England, the more elevated position of the Minister Sahib monopolizing all the attention of the lion-loving public. Colonel Dhere Shum Shere, such was his name, was the most jovial, light-hearted, and thoroughly unselfish being imaginable, brave as a lion, as recent events in Nepaul have proved, always anxious to please, and full of amusing conversation, which, however, from my limited knowledge of Hindostanee, I was unable fully to appreciate.

It is considered a breach of hospitality to make invidious remarks affecting the character of the mansion in which you are a guest; but although my recollections of the Atalanta are most agreeable in reference to the kindness of the officers, I must say she was a most indisputable tub; and if there is an individual who deserves to be turned slowly before the fires in her engine-room, so as to be kept in a state of perpetual blister, it is the Parsee contractor who furnished the provisions, for so meagre was the supply that we could barely satisfy the cravings of hunger.

On the morning of the tenth day after leaving Ceylon we came in sight of the city of palaces, and, sweeping up its magnificent river, soon after anchored amidst a host of other shipping.

Of Calcutta I need say nothing; Chouringhee Road is almost as well known in these days of quick communication as Piccadilly; this is not quite the case with towns in the interior: if it is easy to get to Calcutta, it is not so easy to get beyond, and the means of locomotion by which the traveller makes the journey to Benares are of the most original nature.

The morning of New Year's Day found me comfortably ensconced in a roomy carriage, built almost upon the model of an English stage-coach, in which, with my fellow-traveller, I had passed the night, and which was being dragged along at the rate of about four miles an hour by ten coolies, harnessed to it in what the well-meaning philanthropist of Exeter Hall would call a most barbarous way.

The road along which we were travelling in this extraordinary manner was not, as might be expected, impassable for horses ; on the contrary, it was an excellent macadamized and perfectly level road, denominated the Great Trunk Road of Bengal.

The country through which this road led us was flat, stale, but not unprofitable, since on either side were paddy-fields extending *ad infinitum*, studded here and there with clumps of palms.

The climate was delightful, and the morning air tempted us to uncoil ourselves from our night-wrappers, and take a brisk walk in the dust ; after which we mounted the coach-box, and devised sundry practical methods for accelerating our team, who however were equally ingenious in contriving to save themselves fatigue.

The mid-day sun at last ridded them of their tormentors, and we once more betook ourselves to our comfortable beds in the interior of the conveyance, there to moralize over the barbarism of a man, calling himself an enlightened Englishman, in employing men instead of horses to drag along two of his fellow-countrymen, who showed themselves even more dead to every feeling of humanity by the way in which they urged on their unfortunate fellow-creatures. These coolies were certainly very well paid, and need not have been so employed had they not chosen—for they had all applied for their several appointments—but then the ignominy of the thing!

And so we rolled lazily along, hoping to reach Benares some time within the next fortnight. Before dark we passed through Burdwan, where a few Bengal civilians vegetate on large salaries, to do the work of the rajah, who is still more highly paid not to interfere. He lives magnificently in his palace, and they live magnificently in theirs. We arrived at a small rest-house at night, where we had the satisfaction of eating a fowl in cutlets an hour after it had been enjoying the sweets of life.

There is a considerable amount of enjoyment in suddenly coming to hills after you have for a long time seen nothing but flat country—in first toiling up one and then bowling down the other side, at the imminent peril of the coolies' necks—in seeing streams when you have seen nothing but wells—in coming amidst wood and water and diversified scenery, when every mile that you have travelled for a week past has been the same as the last. Such were our feelings as we woke at daylight one morning in the midst of the Rajmahal hills.

There were a good many carts passing with coal from the Burdwan coal-mines; moreover, we saw sticks, and from the top of each fluttered a little white flag, suggestive of a railway, whereby our present mode of conveyance would be knocked on the head, and all the poor coolies who were pushing us along would be put out of employ. Notwithstanding the disastrous results which must accrue, a railway is really contemplated; but I have heard doubts thrown out as to the present line being the best that could be obtained. It is urged that it has to contend against water carriage—that, with the exception of the Burdwan mines, the coal of which is of an inferior quality, there is no mineral produce—that immense tracts of country through which it passes are totally uncultivated, and from a want of water will in all probability remain so—and it has been calculated that, even if the whole traffic at present passing along the great trunk road of Bengal was to become quadrupled, and if all the Bengal civilians were to travel up and down every day, and various rajahs to take express trains once a week, it would not pay: all these things being considered, were it not that its merits and demerits have been maturely considered by wiser, or at least better informed men than the passing travellers, one might have been inclined to think that those who expressed doubts regarding its success had some good foundation for them.

However, it is better to have a railway on a doubtful line than none at all; the shareholders are guaranteed 5 per cent., and the Government is rich and can afford to pay them. So let us wish success to the experimental railway, and hope that the means of transport may soon be more expeditious than they are at present.

It will doubtless open out the resources of the country, though I cannot but think, for many reasons, that it would have been more judicious to have made the line from Allahabad to Delhi the commencement of the railway system in this part of India, instead of leaving it for a continuation of the line that is now being made.

The bridges we passed over are all on the suspension principle, and do credit to the government; the rivers are difficult to bridge in any other way, as the rains flood them to such an extent that arches will not remain standing for any length of time. It took us two hours to cross the Soan, which we forded or ferried according as the streams between the sand-banks were deep or shallow. This large river is at times flooded to so great an extent that it is one of the most serious obstructions to the railway.

It was not until the morning of the seventh day after leaving Calcutta that we found ourselves on the banks of the Ganges. The Holy City loomed large in the grey dawn of morning, with its tapering minarets barely discernible above it, looking like elongated ghosts.

We were ferried across in a boat of antique construction, better suited for any other purpose than the one to which it was applied, and landed in the midst of the ruins caused by the dreadful explosion of gunpowder that had taken place the previous year: it had occasioned a fearful destruction of property and loss of life, and many hair-breadth escapes were recounted to us. We were told, indeed, that two children, after being buried for five days, were dug out alive; two officers were blown out of the window of an hotel, one of whom was uninjured, the other was only wounded by a splinter, whilst the Kitmutgar, who was drawing a cork close to them at the time, was killed on the spot.

In the course of an hour after leaving this scene of desolation we reached the hospitable mansion which was destined to be our home during our short stay in Benares.

CHAPTER II.

Benares—Cashmere Mull's House—The Chouk—The Bisheshwan Temple, and Maido Rai Minar—Jung Bahadoor in Benares—A Rajah's visit—The marriage of Jung Bahadoor—Review of the Nepaul Rifle Regiment—Benares College.

WHATEVER may be said of the large salaries of the Bengal civilians, they certainly deserve great credit for the praiseworthy employment of their wealth; and making amends as it were for the backwardness of India as regards hotels, they supply their places to the friendless traveller, in a way which our frigid friends at home might imitate with advantage. I look back upon my stay in Benares with the greatest pleasure, and shall long remember the kindness I there experienced.

There is much to be seen in the Holy City, and the means of locomotion which I should recommend the sight-seer to adopt are Tom Johns, or chairs swung upon poles, with or without hoods, as the case may be. Upon arriving at the Chouk or Market-place, we hired two of these conveyances and started to see the residence of Cashmere Mull. But first I must make an attempt, however unsuccessful, to describe the Chouk: it is a large square, studded with raised oblong platforms without walls, the roofs being supported by fluted Ionic columns. The Police Court, in which a Native magistrate presides, forms one side of the square. On the platforms sit the vendors of shawls, skull-caps, toys, shells, sugar-cane, and various other commodities; but to enumerate the extraordinary diversity of goods exposed for sale, or to describe the Babel of tongues which confound the visitor as he wanders through the motley crowd, would be impossible.

We turned out of the Chouk down a narrow street about three feet broad, gloomy from the height of the houses, and unpleasant from the great crowd and close atmosphere; every now and then we got jammed into a corner by some Brahminee bull, who would insist upon standing across the street to eat the fine cauliflower he had just plundered from the stall of an unresisting greengrocer, and who, exercising the proud rights of citizenship, could only be politely coaxed to move his unwieldy carcase out of the way.

We wended our way through pipe bazaars and vegetable bazaars, where each shopkeeper has a sort of stall, with about three feet frontage to the street, but of unknown depth, and a narrow balcony supported by carved wood-work over his head, out of the latticed windows of which bright eyes look down upon the passengers. Whenever there is a piece of wall not otherwise occupied in this compact and busy city, you see depicted, in gaudy colors, elephants rushing along with dislocated joints in hot pursuit of sedate parrots, or brilliant peacocks looking with calm composure upon camels going express, who must inevitably crush them in their headlong career, but the vain birds, apparently taken up with admiration of their own tails, are blind to the impending danger, thereby reading a good lesson both to the passers-by and to the shopkeepers opposite. Now a sudden jerk prevents you from further moralizing, as you find that you are going round a corner so sharp that you must get bumped either before or behind. There are ugly women carrying brass water-vessels, rich merchants on ponies, sirwahs on horses, here and there in the wider streets a camel or an elephant, but very seldom, as few streets would accommodate either of them ; finally there are chuprassies who disperse the crowd with their swords in a most peremptory manner, smiting everything indiscriminately, except the Brahminee bulls, which, although they are much the most serious impediments, are left " alone in their glory."

By the exertions of these city police we reached Cashmere Mull's house, noted as a specimen of antique Oriental architecture.

The court-yard into which we were first ushered reminded me of an old English "hostelrie ;" it was small and uncovered, and round each story ran a curiously worked balcony, on to which opened doors and windows, carved with strange devices, and all the nooks and crannies formed by so much intricate carving were filled with dust and cobwebs. Passing up a narrow, dark, and steep stone stair, we reached a second court-yard, upon the balcony of which we emerged, and which was so very like the last, that I imagined it to be the same, until I remarked that it was smaller, and, if possible, more dirty. We thence ascended to the flat roof of the house, and on our way looked through half-open doors into dark dungeons of rooms, which one would not for the world have ventured into at night.

There was a raised stage with steps up to it, which we ascended and found ourselves on a level with a great many similar stages on the tops of a great many similar houses. A stone parapet about 8 feet high, with beautiful open carving, enclosed this stage, so that we could inspect our neighbours through our stone screen with impunity. On the next roof to where we were was a boy training pigeons, and the numerous crates or frames on the surrounding house-tops showed this to be a favourite amusement. The young gentleman in question certainly made his flock obey him in a wonderful manner, his chief object being to take prisoner a pigeon from his neighbour's flock. He directed their gyrations by loud shrill cries, and, as there were numbers of other members of "Young Benares" employed in like manner, it seemed wonderful how he could recognize his pigeons, or they their master.

Leaving this antique specimen of a nobleman's

town house, we passed through a maze of narrow streets; and bobbing under low archways at the imminent peril of fracturing our skulls, we arrived at the Bisheshwan Temple, which was crowded with Hindoos worshipping the Lingum, representations of which met the eye in every direction.

A well in the yard behind the temple was surrounded by worshippers of the god, who is supposed to have plunged down it and never to have come up again. If so, he must find the smell of decayed vegetation very oppressive, as garlands of flowers and handfuls of rice are continually being offered up, or rather down, to him. From this well we had a good view of the temple, which was covered with gold by Runjeet Singh, and presents a gorgeous and dazzling appearance.

In close vicinity to this temple is a mosque built by Arungzebe to annoy the Hindoos. I ascended the Maido Rai Minar or minaret, and from its giddy height had a magnificent panorama of the city and its environs, with the Ganges flowing majestically beneath, its left bank teeming with life, while the opposite bank seemed desolate.

The observatory, or man mundil, is on the river's bank, and affords a pretty view from its terraces, which are covered with disks and semicircles and magical figures cut in stone.

Gopenate Dore Peshad is the great dealer in Benares embroidery, as well as its manufacturer,

We paid him a visit and were delighted with the rich variety of embroidered goods which were displayed; we saw pieces valued at from 10,000 rupees downwards: magnificent smoking carpets, housings and trappings for horses, shawls, caps, kenkabs, and other articles of eastern attire, were spread out before us in gorgeous profusion. After eating a cardamum, and touching with our pocket-handkerchief some cotton on which had been dropped otto of roses, we ascended to the house-top, and found it built upon much the same plan as Cashmere Mull's, without its antique carving and quaint appearance.

We were not a little glad when the bustle and heat attendant on so much sight-seeing was over, and we forced our way back through the crowded streets.

The population of Benares is estimated by Mr. Prinsep at nearly 200,000; its trade consists chiefly in sugar, saltpetre, indigo, opium, and embroidered cloths; besides which, the city has advantages in its position on the great river, making it, jointly with Mirzapore, the depôt for the commerce of the Dukkum and interior of Hindostan.

General Jung Bahadoor had reached Benares a few days before I arrived there, and I found him installed in a handsome house, the envy of all rajahs, the wonder of the natives, and the admiration of his own countrymen, some thousands of whom had come thus far to meet him. If he had been a *lion* in London, he was not less an object of interest at Benares—his house was always crowded with visitors of high degree, Indian and European ;. one old native rajah in particular was frequently to be seen in close conference with him ; and the result was, that the Prime Minister of Nepaul became the husband of the second daughter of his Highness the ex-Rajah of Coorg. Upon the day following his nuptials my friend and I called upon him, and to our surprise he offered to present us to his newly-wedded bride. We, of course, expressed our sense of the honour he was doing us ; and had just reached the balcony, the stairs leading up to which were on the outside of the house, when our friend the bridegroom perceived his father-in-law, the Coorg rajah, coming in a most dignified manner down the approach. Like a schoolboy caught in the master's orchard, he at once retreated and unceremoniously hurried us back—and just in time, for no doubt, if the old Coorg had detected him thus exhibiting his daughter the day after he had married her, he would have mightily disapproved of so improper a proceeding. This incident shows how utterly Jung despised those prejudices which enthralled his bigoted father-in-law. He was, in fact, the most European Oriental, if I may so speak, that I ever met with, and more thoroughly unaffected and unreserved in his communication with us than is the habit with eastern great men, who always seem afraid of compromising themselves by too much condescension. An instance of this occurred during another visit. While we were chatting on indifferent subjects a native rajah was announced, as being desirous of paying a visit of ceremony. Jung immediately stepped forward to receive him with much politeness. The rajah commenced apologising for not having called sooner, excusing himself on the plea of the present being the only auspicious hour which had been available since his Excellency's arrival; a compliment which the latter returned by remarking that it was unfortunate that his immediate departure would preclude the possibility of his returning his visit, which he the more regretted, as he was at present most particularly engaged in matters of a pressing nature with the English gentlemen, and he therefore hoped he would be excused thus abruptly, but unavoidably, terminating an interview which it would otherwise have given him the greatest pleasure to have prolonged. Thus saying, he politely rose and led the rajah in the most graceful manner to the front door, which was no sooner closed behind him than he returned, rubbing his hands with great glee, as he knowingly remarked, "That is the way to get over an interview with one of these natives."

A detachment of a regiment had come to Benares to escort the General on his journey to Katmandu, and he accordingly determined to favour the inhabitants generally, and the English in particular, with a review.

The men were tall and well-made, and were dressed in a light-green uniform with yellow facings. They went through various evolutions with tolerable regularity; but the performance which excited the most interest was the platoon exercise, no word of command being given, but everything done with the utmost precision at different notes of the music, the men beating time the whole while and giving a swaying motion to their bodies, which produced a most curious effect. The origin of this novel proceeding, his Excellency told us, was a request by the Ranee that some other means should be invented of putting the men through their exercises than by hoarse shouts, which grated upon her ear. The minister immediately substituted this more euphonious but less business-like method.

At this review Jung Bahadoor and his brothers were dressed in the costume they wore when in England: the handsome diamonds in their turbans glittering in the sunshine.

I accompanied him one day on a visit to the Benares college, a handsome building in process of erection by the Indian Government. The Gothic and Oriental styles of architecture are most happily combined, and there is an airiness about the building; but this did not in any way detract from its solidity. The cost of the college and professor's house is not to exceed £13,000; the length of the large school-room is 260 feet, its breadth 35; and there are six large class-rooms on each side.

CHAPTER III.

Jaunpore—A shooting-party—Scenes in camp and on the march—A Nepaulese dinner—Ghazipore—the Company's stud—Indian roads—Passage of the Gograh—Jung Bahadoor's mode of despatching an alligator.

BEING anxious to visit Jaunpore, I left Benares one evening after dinner, and accomplished the distance, 36 miles, with one set of bearers, in seven hours and a half.

The first object that attracts the eye of the traveller as he enters Jaunpore is the many-arched bridge thrown by the Mahometans over the Goomte, and considered the finest built by them in India; on each side are stalls, in which sit the vendors of various wares, after the fashion of old London Bridge. On an island in the middle of the river was discovered a huge figure of a winged lion guarding an elephant, which would suggest some connexion with the sculptures found at Nineveh, and must date much further back than the erection of the bridge.

Passing through a serai, which was filled with travellers, we reached the fort, built, it is supposed, by Khan Kan, or one of the kings of the Shirkee dynasty, about the year 1260. From one of its turrets we had a magnificent view of the town and the surrounding country, while immediately below is seen the river, spanned by the picturesque old bridge, unmoved by the fierce floods which so constantly destroy those arched bridges that have been erected in India by Europeans.

The appearance of the town is diminished in size, but increased in beauty, by the many stately trees which are planted throughout it, while here and there a huge screen of some musjid rears its Egyptian-looking crest, and gives to the town an appearance peculiar to itself; Jaunpore is, in fact, the only city in India in which this style of architecture prevails.

On our way out of the fort we passed a monolithe, on which was an inscription in the same character as that on Ferozeshah's Lath at Delhi, which has been recently translated by Mr. Prinsep. In the main gateway were some porcelain slabs which had at one time formed part of a Jain temple.

The Itala musjid, to which we next bent our steps, has been built on the site of one of these temples; its cloisters remain untouched, and the figures on almost every slab bear undoubted testimony to the previous existence of a Jain temple on this spot. The large square rooms, which were filled during our visit with true believers, were curiously roofed; a dome was ingeniously thrown over the square. An octagon, placed on solid buttresses, supported a 16-sided figure, which in its turn supported the dome. The Jumma musjid, which we also visited, was remarkable for its magnificent screen, 120 feet in height by 70 in breadth, and covered with curious inscriptions and fantastic devices ; the top is slightly narrower than the base, tapering in depth as well as in breadth.

The population of Jaunpore is about 35,000 ; there is a small European station near the town. In the course of the evening's drive I saw a specimen of the Addansonia or baobab-tree : the trunk, measuring 23 feet in circumference, was perfectly smooth and the branches were destitute of leaves. There are but five other specimens in India, and not many in Java, where the tree was discovered by Mr. Addanson ; it is said to have attained, in some instances, the enormous age of 2000 years.

Leaving Jaunpore about midnight, I reached the camp of Jung Bahadoor on the following day. The scene as we approached was in the highest degree picturesque ; 5000 Nepaulese were here collected, followers, in various capacities, of the Prime Minister, whose tents were pitched at a little distance from the grove of mango-trees which sheltered his army and retainers. On our arrival he was out shooting, so, mounting an elephant, we proceeded to join him. We heard such frequent reports of fire-arms that we fully expected to find excellent sport ; great was my disappointment, therefore, when I saw him surrounded by some 20 or 30 followers, who held umbrellas, loaded his guns, rushed to pick up the *game*, or looked on applaudingly while he stealthily crept up to take a deliberate pot shot at some unlucky parrot or some bird that might catch his eye as it perched on a branch, or fluttered unconsciously amongst the leaves. But the most interesting object in the group was the lately-wedded bride, who was seated in a howdah. Jung introduced her to me as "his beautiful Missis"—a description she fully deserved. She was very handsome, and reflected much credit on the taste of the happy bridegroom, who seemed pleased when we expressed our approval of his choice.

Before quitting the subject of Jung's shooting-party, I must remark, in justice to him as a sportsman, that he considers nothing less than a deer to be game at all. Tiger or rhinoceros shooting is his favorite sport, and he looks upon shooting a parrot, a snipe, a hawk, or a partridge as being equally unworthy of the name of sport, nor does he understand why some of those birds should be dignified with the name of "game," and the others not.

At dawn on the following morning the stir and bustle in camp announced an early start, and our elephant appeared at the tent door just as the gallant rifle corps marched past, the band playing the "British Grenadiers." Mounting the elephant, we picked our way through the débris of the camp, now almost deserted; some few of the coolies were still engaged packing the conical baskets which they carry on their backs, one strap passing over the forehead, and two others over the shoulders. The appearance of a hill coolie as he thus staggers along under his tremendous burden is singular enough, and so totally unlike that of the coolies of the plains, that it was a sort of promise of there being in store for us more curiosities, both of Nepaulese men and manners, in their native country, and we looked with no little interest upon the first specimens we had seen of the Newar race—the aborigines of Nepaul. Short and compact, the full development of their muscle bore evidence to their almost Herculean strength. Their flat noses, high cheek-bones, small eyes, and copper-colored complexion are unequivocal signs of a Mongolian origin, whilst the calves of their legs, which I never saw equalled in size, indicate the mountainous character of their country.

Threading our way on our wary elephant through nearly 5000 of these singular-looking beings, all heavily loaded with the appurtenances of the camp, we soon overtook the cortège of the Minister and his brothers, which consisted of three or four carriages dragged along by coolies, over a road which, in many places, must have severely tried the carriage springs, as well as nearly dislocated the joints of Jung's "beautiful little Missis," whom I saw peeping out of one of the windows. The rest of this motley crowd, with which we were destined to march for the next three weeks, was made up of Nepaul gentlemen in various capacities, who cantered past on spirited little horses, or squatted cross-legged in the clumsy, oddly constructed " Ecce," a sort of native gig ; besides these, there were merchants and peddlers, who followed the camp as a matter of speculation. Amidst an indiscriminate horde, our elephant jogged lazily along, generally surrounded by eight or ten others, with whom we marched for company's sake. We usually arrived at the mango tope destined to be our camping-ground about ten o'clock in the morning, and lounged away the heat of the day in tents ; towards the afternoon Jung generally went out with his gun or rifle, shooting with the former at parrots at ten yards distance, and with the latter at bottles at a hundred. There was not much attraction for the sportsman throughout the whole line of march, and I only bagged a few couple of snipe, partridges, wild-duck, and quail.

Our dinner was always supplied from Jung's own carpet, for he does not use a table, and it was with no little curiosity that at the end of the first day's march I looked forward to the productions of a Nepaul cuisine. We had not forgotten to provide ourselves with a sufficient *stand-by* in case it should not prove altogether palatable. Towards evening an enormous dish, containing rice enough to have satisfied the whole of the gallant rifle corps, was brought into our tent, closely followed by about 20 little cups formed of leaves, one inside the other, each containing about a thimbleful of some exquisite condiment; also three or four saucers containing some cold gravy, of unpleasant color, in which floated about six minute particles of meat.

Filling my plate with rice, which had been well and carefully greased to improve its flavor, and scientifically mixing the various other ingredients therewith, I unhesitatingly launched a spoonful into my mouth, when I was severely punished for my temerity, and almost overcome by the detestable compound of tastes and smells that at once assailed both nose and palate: it was a pungent, sour, bitter, and particularly greasy mouthful; but what chiefly astonished me, so much as to prevent my swallowing it for some time, was the perfume of Colonel Dhere Shum Shere, the fat brother, which I was immediately sensible of, as overpowering everything else. Not that I would for a moment wish to insinuate that it was a nasty smell; on the contrary, it would have been delicious on a pocket-handkerchief; but to imagine it going down one's throat, in company with an immense amount of grease and gravy, was nearly enough to prevent its doing so at all.

Our march to Ghazipore was through country richly cultivated and pleasing, if not absolutely pretty. The numerous poppy-plantations were evidence of our proximity to the head-quarters of one of the largest opium agencies in India. Ghazipore is approached by an avenue of handsome trees, more ornamental than useful, seeing how utterly destructive it is to the permanent welfare of a road.

The mausoleum, containing a monument to Lord Cornwallis, is solid but not ungraceful: upon one side of the monument are sculptured the figures of a Hindoo and a Mussulman, and on the other a British and a native grenadier, all of whom are weeping. The building is prettily situated near the bank of the Ganges, on a large plain or maidan, across which pleasant avenues lead in all directions; the one which we followed brought us to the stables of the Company's stud, containing 700 horses. On our way we remarked a number of handsome houses now unoccupied and falling rapidly into decay, the military force at the station having of late been much reduced. The horses were being exercised, notwithstanding which they carried a good deal of superfluous fat, and vented their spirits by occasionally breaking loose, and dashing pellmell through rings of their companions, who, grudging them the sweets of liberty, made vigorous efforts to partake of them, and in some instances succeeded. I saw not less than eight at once dashing about in the large training enclosure. My friend having already bought three, we thought it best to withdraw ourselves from further temptation, and set out to join the camp at Cossimabad, 16 miles distant, still passing through richly cultivated country, which was as pretty as a dead level ever can be.

The crops most generally reared are, sugar-cane, poppies, rare (a species of pulse), wheat often with a delicate border of blue-flowered flax, tobacco, mustard, peas, and sometimes vetches. The large rose-gardens for which Ghazipore is celebrated lay to the right. I regretted that our way did not lead us through them, but we had evidence of their existence in some delicious otto of roses, which is easily procured here.

The road by which we were now travelling was what is called in India a cutcher-road, which means unmetalled. It is a pity that Government should spend so much in macadamizing roads, when cutcher-roads answer just as well for all the wants of native traffic. The rocks here are of limestone formation, and consequently, as there is not much traffic on any road in India, if the trees were cut down, roads on a limestone formation would always keep themselves in repair, provided the side drains were properly kept open. The bridges are all good, and, if the line of road was well bridged throughout, the country conveyances could always make their way along it with perfect ease. If the money now spent in macadamizing were spent in making the necessary bridges, the resources of the country would be much more fully opened out than they are at present; a garre-waller, or cart-man, can always appreciate a bridge, never a macadamized road. At present the bridges on this road are all wooden, and liable to be carried away by the first heavy flood.

The whole way to the frontier of Nepaul we travelled along a cutcher-road, accompanied by a train of at least a hundred hackerys, without the slightest inconvenience; and until the style of cart at present used by the natives becomes wonderfully improved, this road may well be used, except of course during the rains.

A few days' march brought us to the banks of the Gograh, a large river rising in the western Terai, and measuring, at the point where we crossed, at least half a mile in breadth. As we came upon the cliff overlooking the river, the scene was novel and amusing. As 5000 persons had to reach the opposite bank, and no preparations had been made for their transit, the confusion may be easily imagined. The good-humour of the hillmen, however, was imperturbable, and, though there was plenty of loud talking, the remarks made were usually of a facetious nature.

The stream was rapid, and carried the boats down some distance. Ten elephants, with nothing visible but the tips of their trunks and the crowns of their heads, on which latter squatted the mahouts, made the passage gallantly. On the opposite side we passed through a village, the little square of which was absolutely filled with monkeys. They resort thither by hundreds from the neighbouring jungles to be fed by the villagers, and are most independent in their behaviour, unscrupulously attacking the man who brings their daily allowance, and, as they are accounted sacred, they are of course unmolested. We saw some serious fights amongst them, young and old mixing indiscriminately in the mêlée ; a mother was frequently seen making a rapid but orderly retreat with her young one on her back.

We occasionally passed picturesque villages, the inhabitants of which were of course all attracted by so novel a spectacle. The system pursued by the villagers here is the same as may be observed in many parts of the Continent of Europe : they invariably congregate in a collection of mud-built closely packed huts, showing a gregarious disposition, and great aversion to living alone. I do not remember to have passed one solitary house. As the whole of the country is richly cultivated, the distance of their dwellings from the scene of their daily labour must in some instances be considerable.

The Gandaki, over which we were ferried, is a large stream rising in Nepaul, and as broad as the Gograh. We went some distance up its banks, in the hopes of finding wild-pig, but were unsuccessful.

The minister, however, being determined not to go home empty handed, doomed to destruction a huge alligator, unconsciously basking on a sand-bank. Accordingly, arming eight of us with double-barrelled rifles, he marched us in an orderly manner to the bank, when, at a given signal, 16 balls whistled through the air, arousing in a most unpleasant manner the monster from his mid-day slumbers, who plunged into the stream and disappeared almost instantaneously, and the Minister Sahib, coolly pulling out the wallet which contained his tiffin, remarked that we might profitably employ ourselves in that way until he came up to breathe, when he should receive another dose. Retiring therefore a few yards from me—for a Hindoo may not eat in the presence of a Christian—he and his brothers were soon deep in the mysteries of curious viands. Perceiving, however, that I was not prepared for an alfresco luncheon, he shared with me some grapes, pomegranates, &c., as well as a piece of green-looking meat, which I found very delightfully scented. As we were in the middle of our repast, our wounded friend showed his nose above the water, when he was immediately struck by a splendid shot from the minister, who was in no way disconcerted by having his mouth full at the time. Lashing the water furiously with his tail, the alligator once more disappeared : he came up shortly after, and the same scene was enacted three times before his huge form floated lifeless down the stream.

CHAPTER IV.

A picnic on the Nepaul frontier—A boar-hunt—The Terai and its resources—Our shooting quarters—Incidents of sport—A tiger-hunt—The great elephant exhibition of 1851—Camp Bechiacor.

PITCHED under the shade of some wide-spreading mangoes are a variety of tents of all sizes, from the handsome and spacious marquee to the snug sleeping tent; near them are picqueted a number of fine-looking Arab horses in prime condition, while the large barouche, which is standing close by, might have just emerged from a coach-house in a London mews; a few servants are loitering about, and give life to this otherwise tranquil scene.

Nobody can for an instant suppose that this is the camp of Jung Bahadoor; his tents are green and red, and generally surrounded by soldiers; his horses do not look so sleek and fresh as these; he has not got a barouche belonging to him, far less a piano, and I think I hear the music of one proceeding from yonder large tent.—No—this is an Indian picnic—none of your scrambling, hurried pleasure parties to last for a wet day, when everybody brings his own food, and eats it uncomfortably with his fingers, with some leaves for a plate and an umbrella for a roof, and then persuades himself and others that he has been enjoying himself. Let such an one come and make trial of a deliberate, well-organized picnic of a fortnight's duration, such as the one now before us, with plenty of sport in the neighbourhood, while the presence of the fair sex in camp renders the pleasures of the drawing-room doubly delightful after those of the chace.

Boar-hunting, or, as it is commonly called, pig-sticking, is essentially an Indian sport, and I could not have partaken of it under more favourable auspices than I did at Hirsede, when, having obtained intelligence of a wild boar, and having been supplied with steeds, some five or six of us proceeded in pursuit of the denizen of the jungles. We soon roused and pressed him closely through the fields of castor-oil and rarecates. The thick stalks of the former often balked our aim. He received repeated thrusts notwithstanding, and charged three or four times viciously, slightly wounding my horse, and more severely that of one of my companions. After being mortally wounded, the brute unfortunately dodged into a thick jungle, where, hiding himself in the bushes, he baffled all our efforts to dislodge him. In their attempts to do so, however, the beaters turned out a fine young boar, who gave us a splendid run of upwards of a mile at top speed—for a pig is a much faster animal than his appearance indicates, and one would little imagine, as he scuttles along, that he could keep a horse at full gallop. However, he soon became blown, and, no friendly patch of jungle being near for him to take refuge in, was quickly despatched.

Our revels having been kept up to a late hour, I left Hirsede in the small hours of the morning, and came up to Jung Bahadoor's camp on the Nepaul frontier.

A small stream divides the Company's from the Nepaulese dominions, and on crossing it the change of government was at once obvious. The villages looked more wretched, the people more dirty, the country was almost totally uncultivated, and nearly all traces of roads disappeared as we traversed the green sward of the Terai of Nepaul, scattered over which were large herds of cattle, grazing on the short grass, which extended in all directions over the vast expanse of flat country.

This province is governed by Krishna Bahadoor, a younger brother of the prime minister, an active and energetic officer. Any complaint of the peasantry is in the first instance brought to his notice, and referred by him to his rother, if his decision does not give satisfaction. His subordinates are a sirdar, or judge, and several subahs, or collectors.

The Terai is a long, narrow strip of territory, extending for three hundred miles along the northern frontier of British India, and is about twenty miles in breadth. The whole tract is a dead level. For the first ten miles after crossing the frontier the country is used chiefly for grazing by the inhabitants of the adjoining British provinces, who drive thousands of cattle across the border, paying a considerable revenue to the Nepaul government for the privilege of so doing.

Ten miles from the frontier commences the great saul forest, which is also ten miles in breadth. It is composed almost entirely of the valuable saul-tree and a great quantity of timber is annually exported to Calcutta down the Gandaki, which is navigable to the foot of the Cheriagotty hills. The licence to fell the saul timber is confined exclusively to Nepaul merchants, and the payment demanded by Government for such permission is so enormous that the trade is not very profitable.

The principal sources of revenue derived from this district are the land-tax and the receipts from the sale of licences for felling timber and for grazing cattle. The large amount thus received, together with the number of elephants which are annually caught in the great forest, renders the Terai a most valuable appendage to the Nepaul dominions.

It is, however, entirely owing to the excellent management of Jung that the revenue of the Terai is now so considerable. In 1816 this province did not yield more than one-tenth its present revenue, which is now computed to amount to fifty lacs (500,000*l.*). Still the Terai might be made yet more profitable. At present no use whatever is made of the hides and horns of the hundreds of head of cattle that die daily in this district, which are left to rot on the carcases of the beasts. It would remain to be proved however whether, even if permission were granted by the Nepaul Government, any would be found possessing the capital or enterprise to engage in a speculation which would, unquestionably, ensure a handsome return.

It is not, however, in a pecuniary point of view alone that the Terai is considered by the Nepaulese as contributing to the prosperity of their dominions; it is looked upon as one of their chief safeguards against invasion. For nine or ten months a disease, denominated by the natives the "Ayul," renders the Terai impassable to man, so deadly are its effects even to the natives of the country. It would appear that might be obviated—if we are to believe the native theory somewhat gravely recorded by Mr. Hamilton (who made a journey through this province with a mission sent by Government in 1803) by going in search of and killing certain serpents, which are said to poison the atmosphere with their breath. I should be inclined to recommend the cutting down of the jungle in preference to the cutting up of the serpents; and I have little doubt that, were parts of the great forest cleared, and wide roads cut through it, it would cease to be so pestilential a locality as it is at present. In case of a war, there would be no difficulty, even now, in our troops possessing themselves of the whole territory to the foot of the Cheriagotty hills in the cold season; but as we should have to maintain some position throughout the year, the top of those hills themselves would be the only one available, and here, in the heart of an enemy's country, and cut off from all communication with India, the position of the garrison would be anything but enviable.

I observed several of the natives of this district afflicted with goître, and I was informed that cretinism was also prevalent,—a fact which proves clearly the fallacy of the old doctrine that these complaints are attributable to snow-water, for all the water drunk by the inhabitants of the Terai rises in the Cheriagotty hills, on which snow rarely if ever falls. This would be strongly corroborative of the correctness of the idea that malaria is the origin of goître and cretinism, even if the experiment which has been tried at Interlacken, of building a hospital on the hills, above the influence of the infectious atmosphere in the valley, had not proved completely successful.

The camp which was destined to be our head-quarters during a few days' shooting was pitched in the plain near the village of Bisoleah, distant about two miles from the borders of the grand jungle. Its appearance was totally different from those already described; two more regiments were here in attendance upon the Minister; the men were all comfortably lodged in grass huts got up for the occasion, and the innumerable host of camp followers, who on the march had been contented with wrapping themselves up in their thick cloths, and sleeping in groups round the various fires, were now engaged in erecting like temporary habitations, forming by these means a grass village of considerable extent.

Horses, oxen, camels, elephants, were tethered in every direction, or wandering in search of sweeter tufts of grass. The village itself was close and dirty; the largest house, which stood near a temple, was occupied by some half-dozen wives of the Minister, who had come to the borders of their country to welcome home their lord and master.

Our tents were pitched between the camp and a small clump of trees, near which upwards of 300 elephants were tethered; a stream divided us from them, the banks of which presented a continual scene of confusion, as men and animals, at all hours, passed along in crowds, while the motley groups, collecting as the Minister moved about to inspect various parts of his establishment, indicated the whereabouts of that great personage. The scene struck us as particularly novel and attractive when we arrived from Hersede about mid-day; as we approached from one direction, the Minister Sahib arrived from another, mounted in a handsome howdah, the trophy of the morning being a tiger which he had just killed, and which was lashed on to the elephant following him, while a hundred more hustled one another up the steep bank and through the crowded street, greatly to the inconvenience of his dutiful subjects, who were salaaming vociferously.

We immediately started in quest of like game, and commenced beating the heavy jungle, by which the plain was bounded as by a wall, but fortune did not smile upon our efforts, and we only succeeded in killing a deer and a pig. I found my first experience in shooting from a howdah to be anything but agreeable : the deer bounds through the long grass as a rabbit would through turnips ; and, at the moment one catches a glimpse of his head, the elephant is sure to be going down a steep place, or stopping or going on suddenly, or trumpeting, or doing something which completely balks a sportsman accustomed to be on his own legs, and sends the ball flying in any direction but the right one. Our line of elephants consisted of upwards of one hundred, and they beat regularly and silently enough, except when the behavior of one of them irritated some passionate mahout, who would vent his wrath upon the head of the animal by a blow from a short iron rod, or would catch him sharply under the ear with a huge hook, which he dexterously applied to a sore kept open for that purpose; then a loud roar of pain would sound through the jungle for a moment, much to our disgust, as it startled the deer we were silently and gradually approaching.

The pig, which formed part of the game-bag of the afternoon, was, in the first instance, only severely wounded, and an elephant was commanded to finish the poor brute; as he lay, grimly surveying us, his glistening tusks looked rather formidable,—so at least the elephant seemed to think, as for some time he strongly objected to approach him. At last he went timidly up and gave the boar a severe kick with his fore-foot, drawing it back quickly with a significant grunt, which plainly intimated his opinion that he had done as much as could reasonably be expected of him. His mahout, however, thought otherwise, and by dint of severe irritation on the sore behind his ear, seemed to drive him to desperation, as the elephant suddenly backed upon the pig, and, getting him between his hind legs, ground them together, and absolutely broke him up. After this we went crashing home, regardless of the thick jungle through which we passed, as the impending boughs were snapped, at the word of the mahouts, by the obedient and sagacious animals they bestrode.

Daybreak of the 30th of January found us not foot in stirrup, but foot on ladder, for we were mounting our elephants to proceed in search of the monarch of the Indian jungles, intelligence of the lair of a male and female having been brought into camp overnight. A hundred elephants followed in a line, forming a picturesque procession, towards the long grass jungle in which our noble game was reported to be ensconced. On reaching the scene of action we formed into a line and beat regularly the whole length of the patch. We were not destined to wait long, and the crack of my friend's rifle soon sounded in my ears. He had wounded the tiger severely, and the animal had again disappeared in the long grass. We were now on the alert, as it was impossible he could escape us; and in a few moments I had the satisfaction of seeing him bounding through the grass at about thirty yards' distance. The report of my rifle was quickly followed by three more shots as he passed down the line, and he fell dead at the feet of the Minister, with five balls in his body.

In the evening, after our return from a good day's sport, we paid Jung Bahadoor a visit in his tent, and went with him to see the elephants which had been caught for the service of the Government during his year's absence from the country. In a square enclosure were upwards of two hundred elephants of all sorts and sizes. Here might be seen an elephant fastened between two others, and kept quiet only by being dragged continually in two different directions at once, no mahout having yet ventured to mount him; while, in evident terror at her proximity to such a monster, stood an anxious mother performing maternal duties to a young one not much larger than a calf, who was in no way puzzled by the position of the udder between her fore-legs, but by a dexterous use of his trunk helped himself in a manner wonderfully precocious for so young a baby; indeed, he seemed very much pleased with having a trunk to play with, and certainly had a great advantage over most babies in possessing so permanent a plaything. Behind this interesting party stood a large elephant, with huge tusks, which had been chiefly instrumental in the capture of the victims he was now grimly surveying at a considerable distance, it not being safe to let him approach too near, as he seemed to be under the delusion that every elephant he saw still required to be caught. Each mahout now brought forward the prizes he had captured since the commencement of the year, and they were severally inspected: those which had no tufts of hair at the tips of their tails, or were in any way deformed, were put aside to be sold to unwary purchasers in India; while those approved by his Excellency were reserved for the use of government, or, to speak in plainer language, for his shooting parties.

As I do not know the points of an elephant as well as those of a horse, the want of the tuft was the only mark I could distinguish. However, the science of elephant-flesh seemed to be as deep and full of mysteries as that of horse-flesh.

Having finished our inspection, and the pay of an unsuccessful mahout or two having been stopped, Jung entered into a long disquisition upon the subject of the wild sports of the Terai. He told us, amongst other things, that he had forbidden all deer-shooting here, although the revenue to Government upon the skins amounted to 400*l.* or 500*l.* a year, in order that he might enjoy better shooting. Of course, we praised the love of sport which could prompt such an order, and said nothing of the love of country which might perhaps have prevented it. I was often struck by the despotic tone which the prime minister assumed, and it only confirmed my previous opinion as to his substantially possessing the sovereign power.

We killed five or six more deer and pigs before quitting Bisoleah on the following day, our road to Bechiacor leading us through the great forest, at this season perfectly healthy. We found our camp pitched in the broad dry bed of a mountain torrent, which I observed to be filled with fragments of granite and micacious schist.

As the shades of evening closed in upon the valley, the scene became extremely interesting: high upon the hill sides,—for we had reached the base of the Cheriagotty hills,—groups of natives, crouching round their fires, were sheltered only by grass huts, the labour of an hour.

While lights twinkled in the minister's camp, soldiers were gathered round their watch-fires, and the villagers were assembled near a huge crackling blaze to witness so unusual, and to them so exciting a scene, as 5000 souls encamped in their solitary valley.

CHAPTER V.

March to Hetowra—Cross the Cheriagotty Hills—Scenes of the war of 1815-16—Preparations for a wild elephant hunt—The herd in full cry—A breakneck country—Furious charges of wild elephants—The lost child—Return to camp.

EARLY on the following morning we were on the march, and for five miles did our clumsy elephant trip it heavily over the large stones forming the bed of the stream in which we had been encamped the previous night. I fear the beauty of the scenery did not so well compensate him for the badness of the road as his more fortunate riders. To see a hill at a distance after having travelled so long over a dead level was refreshing; but when we began to wind round the base of precipitous cliffs, or clamber up some romantic mountain pass, the effect was most animating.

The cliffs which now frowned over us were about 500 feet in height; a few larches crowning the summit indicated the elevation of the country, and almost reminded us of home, until some monkeys swinging about amongst the branches at once dispelled the illusion.

The hills themselves consist entirely of clay mixed with sandstone, mica, and gravel; and the effect of the mountain torrents during the rainy season upon such soft material had been to form precipitous gullies, along which we were now passing, while the grotesque pinnacles which constantly met the eye reminded us of the dolomite formation of the Tyrol. In many places were strata, sometimes horizontal, but more frequently inclined at an angle of about forty-five degrees, consisting of limestone, hornstone, and conglomerate.

This range is called by Hodgson the sandstone range; it does not rise more than 600 feet from its immediate base, its elevation above the sea being about 3000 feet. The pass itself, by which we crossed the Cheriagotty hills, was a mere water-course, sometimes so narrow that the banks on each side might be touched from the back of the elephant, and so steep and rocky that, both in ascending and descending into the dry bed of a torrent, the animal found no little difficulty in keeping his footing.

It was in this place that some of the severest fighting took place in 1816 during the Nepaulese war. Commanded by the surrounding heights and crowned by the temporary stockades of the Ghorkas, it was a dangerous and formidable obstacle to the progress of our army; but the able tactics of Sir David Ochterlony successfully overcame it. In the very watercourse we were now traversing the carcase of a dead elephant had, on one occasion during that campaign, fallen in such a manner as effectually to block up the way; and so narrow is the path, and so steep the banks on each side, that the army was absolutely delayed some time until this cumbrous impediment was removed.

After descending into the bed of the Chyria Nuddee our road lay through the saul forest, the magnificent trees of which served as a grateful shade for some miles, while, the road being comparatively level and free from impediments, our journey was most agreeable. A short distance from our destination we crossed the Kurroo Nuddee, by a picturesque wooden bridge peculiar to the Himalayas.

Hetowra is a place of considerable importance in a mercantile point of view, but it is not gay except during the season; it is, in fact, fashionable only while it is healthy. From this place two roads lead to Katmandu. The whole of our week's stay in the Terai was rendered interesting to us from the recollection that in this province originated a war as disastrous to our troops as it was unprovoked by us. Never in our eastern experience have we commenced hostilities with a native power upon more justifiable grounds, and seldom have we paid more dearly for the satisfaction of at last dictating terms, from which indeed we have since reaped no great advantage. At Persa, but a short distance from Bisoleah, Captain Sibley and his detachment fell into the hands of the enemy, losing two guns and three-fourths of his men.

Major-General Gillespie fell at the storming of Kalunga, while gallantly cheering on his men; our casualties here amounting to 225, twenty of whom were officers. Beaten back on this occasion, we were no less unsuccessful in a second attempt, losing in killed and wounded 483 men, including eleven officers. It was only when General Ochterlony assumed the command that affairs began to wear a brighter aspect. The energy and ability of this officer were displayed in a series of operations which daunted the enemy in proportion as they inspired confidence amongst our own ranks, and the result of the campaign was the expulsion of the Ghorkas from a large tract of country, which was subsequently annexed to British India. Attempts at negotiation were then made, which ultimately proved futile, and after the usual amount of delay, specious professions, and deceit common to native Courts generally had been practised by the Nepaul Durbar with a view to gain time, open hostilities broke out with redoubled vigour on both sides. General Ochterlony assumed the command of an army of 36,000 men and commenced the campaign by moving the main body at once across the Cheriagotty hills, an operation involving incredible toil and difficulty, but which was, nevertheless, performed with the greatest rapidity. From Hetowra he advanced upon Muckwanpore, which, after two engagements, fell into his hands, our loss amounting to nearly 300. This fort commands the valley of Katmandu, and the Durbar therefore thought it advisable to treat as speedily as possible. The terms which were finally agreed upon differed little from those proposed on the former occasion, leaving in our hands a portion of the Terai, and, what was more important, giving the Ghorkas a more correct notion of the enemy they had to deal with than they had gained from their experience in the first campaign.

We found our camp prettily situated at the village of Hetowra, on the Rapti, surrounded by hills clothed to their summits with evergreen jungle not unlike those I had lately left in Ceylon.

The Minister Sahib, having received information that a herd of wild elephants were in the neighbourhood, paid us a visit immediately on our arrival at camp, in a great state of excitement, and enjoined on us the necessity of an early start if we wished to partake of a sport which he promised would exceed anything we had ever witnessed, and prove such as no European had ever before had an opportunity of joining in.

I was aroused about 3 on the following morning, by the tune of the 'British Grenadiers,' played by the bands of the two regiments, which marched past my tent on their way to beat the jungle, and I wondered whether its composer ever imagined that its inspiriting effects would be exercised upon men bound on so singular a duty as those whose tramp we now heard becoming fainter and fainter as they wound up the valley. This was a signal for us to abandon our mattresses, which were always spread on the ground, in default of a four-poster, but were none the less comfortable or fascinating to their drowsy occupants on that account. It was necessary to make such a morning's meal as should be sufficient to last for 24 hours. This was rather a difficult matter at that early hour, as we had eaten a large dinner over-night; however, we accomplished it to the best of our power, and, jumping into our howdah, soon overtook Jung, whom we accompanied to what was to be the scene of action, a thick saul jungle on the banks of the Curroo Nuddee, here a considerable stream.

Down a hill before us, and by a particular pass, the wild elephants were to be driven by the united efforts of the gallant rifle corps, a regiment of infantry, and a hundred elephants; while our party, which comprised an equal number of these animals, was prepared to receive their brethren of the woods.

Our patience as sportsmen was destined to be severely tried, and mid-day came without any elephants having made their appearance: we therefore lit a huge fire, and, dismounting, partook with Jung of some very nice sweet biscuits and various specimens of native confectionery, declining the green-looking mutton which was kindly pressed upon us. Had the elephants chosen that moment to come down upon us, a curious scene must have ensued : Jung's grapes would have gone one way and his curry-powder the other—he was eating grapes and curry-powder at the time ; and his brother, who was toasting a large piece of mutton on a reed, must have either burnt his mouth or lost the precious morsel : however, the elephants did not come, so Jung finished his grapes and curry-powder, and his brother waited till the mutton was cool, ate it in peace, and went through the necessary ablutions. He then gave me a lesson in cutting down trees with a kukri, a sort of bill-hook, in the use of which the Nepaulese are peculiarly expert. The Minister Sahib at one stroke cut through a saul-tree which was 13 inches in circumference, while sundry unsuccessful attempts which I made on very small branches created great amusement among the by-standers skilled in the use of the weapon.

At last a dropping shot or two were heard in the distance: this was the signal of the approach of the herd, and I was put by the minister through the exercises necessary to be acquired before commencing the novel chace.

Taking off my shoes and tying a towel round my head, I was told to suppose an immense branch to be in front of me, and was taught to escape its sweeping effects by sliding down the crupper of the elephant, and keeping the whole of my body below the level of his back, thus allowing the branch to pass within an inch above it without touching me. In the same manner, upon a branch threatening me from the right or left, it was necessary to throw myself on the opposite side, hanging only by my hands, and swinging myself into my original position by a most violent exertion, which required at the same time considerable knack. Having perfected myself in these accomplishments to the utmost of my power, I awaited in patience the arrival of the elephants.

Looking round, I saw Jung himself, seated in the place of the mahout, guiding the elephant which he bestrode very cleverly. When silence was required he made a peculiar clucking noise with his tongue; whereupon these docile creatures immediately became still and motionless: one would drop the tuft of grass which he was tearing up, another would stop instantly from shaking the dust out of the roots which he was preparing to eat, others left off chewing their food. When a few seconds of the most perfeet calm had elapsed, the rooting up and dusting out went on more briskly than ever, and the mouthful was doubly sweet to those who were now allowed to finish the noisy process of mastication.

At last our patience was rewarded, and Jung gave the signal for us to advance.

On each elephant there were now two riders, the mahout and a man behind, who, armed with a piece of hard wood into which two or three spikes were inserted, hammered the animal about the root of the tail as with a mallet. He was furnished with a looped rope to hold on by, and a sack stuffed with straw to sit upon, and was expected to belabour the elephant with one hand while he kept himself on its back with the other.

This was the position I filled on this trying occasion ; but my elephant fared well as regarded the instrument of torture, for I was much too fully occupied in taking care of myself to think of using it. Away we went at full speed, jostling one another up banks and through streams, and I frequently was all but jolted off the diminutive sack which ought to have formed my seat, but did not, for I found it impossible to sit. Being quite unable to maintain any position for two moments together, I looked upon it as a miracle that every bone in my body was not broken. Sometimes I was suddenly jerked into a sitting posture, and, not being able to get my heels from under me in time, they received a violent blow. A moment after I was thrown forward on my face, only righting myself in time to see a huge impending branch, which I had to escape by slipping rapidly down the crupper, taking all the skin off my toes in so doing, and, what would have been more serious, the branch nearly taking my head off if I did not stoop low enough. When I could look about me, the scene was most extraordinary and indescribable: a hundred elephants were tearing through the jungle as rapidly as their unwieldy forms would let them, crushing down the heavy jungle in their headlong career, while their riders were gesticulating violently, each man punishing his elephant, or making a bolster of himself as he flung his body on one side or the other to avoid branches; while some, Ducrow-like, and confident in their activity, were standing on the bare backs of their elephants, holding only by the looped rope,—a feat I found easy enough in the open country, but fearfully dangerous in the jungle. A few yards in front of us was a wild elephant with her young one, both going away in fine style, the pace being 8 or 9 miles an hour. I was just beginning to appreciate the sport, and was contemplating hammering my elephant so as to be up amongst the foremost, when we, in company with about half a dozen others, suddenly disappeared from the scene. A nullah, or deep drain, hidden in the long grass, had engulfed elephants and riders. The suddenness of the shock unseated me, but fortunately I did not lose my hold of the rope, and more fortunately still my elephant did not roll over, but, balancing himself on his knees, with the assistance of his trunk, made a violent effort, and succeeded in getting out of his uncomfortable position.

The main body of the chase had escaped this

nullah by going round the top of it; but we were not so much thrown out as I expected, for we arrived in time to see the wild elephant charging and struggling in the midst of her pursuers, who, after several attempts, finally succeeded in noosing her, and dragging her away in triumph between two tame elephants, each attached to the wild one by a rope, and pulling different ways whenever she was inclined to be unmanageable. I was watching the struggles which the huge beast made, and wondering how the young one, who was generally almost under the mother, had escaped being crushed in the mêlée, when a perfect roll of small arms turned our attention to another quarter, and I saw an elephant with an imposing pair of tusks charging down upon us through a square of soldiers, which had just been broken by it, and who were now taking to the trees in all directions. I ought to remark, lest the gallant riflemen should be under the imputation of want of valour in this proceeding, that they were only allowed to fire blank cartridge. The elephant next to me stood the brunt of the charge, which was pretty severe, while mine created a diversion by butting him violently in the side, and, being armed with a formidable pair of tusks, made a considerable impression; the wild one was soon completely overpowered by numbers, after throwing up his trunk and charging wildly in all directions. Of the violence of one of these charges I have retained visible proof, for a splintered tusk, which had been broken short off in the combat, was afterwards picked up and given to me as a trophy. Having succeeded in noosing this elephant also, we were dragging him away in the usual manner between two others, when he snapped one of the ropes and started off, pulling after him the elephant that still remained attached to him, and dashed through the jungle at full speed, notwithstanding the struggles of the involuntary companion of his flight. For a moment I feared that the courage of the mahout would give way in that pell-mell career, and that he would slip the rope which bound the two animals together. But he held on manfully, and after another exciting chace we succeeded in surrounding the maddened monster; my elephant jostled him so closely that I could touch him as we went neck and neck. It is a curious fact that the elephants never seem to think of uncurling their trunks, and sweeping their persecutors from the backs of their tame brethren: this they have never been known to do, though it has not unfrequently occurred that a wild herd have proved more than a match for the tame one, and then there is nothing for it but to turn and make off in an ignominious retreat as fast as the blows of the mahouts can urge them. It is only under these circumstances that there is any danger to the riders, and such an occurrence can take place only when the tame herd is small, and encounters an unusually large number of the wild elephants. Upon this occasion we mustered so strong that defeat was out of the question.

We now heard a terrific bellowing at a short distance, which, in my ignorance, I thought proceeded from a huge tusker making a gallant resistance somewhere ; I was rather disappointed, therefore, to find that the object of interest to a large group of men and elephants was only a young one struggling on his back in a deep hole into which he had fallen, and from which he was totally unable to extricate himself. Lying on his back, and kicking his legs wildly about in the air, he looked the most ridiculous object imaginable, and certainly made more noise in proportion to his size than any baby I ever heard. So incessant was his roaring that we could scarcely hear each other speak ; at last, by means of ropes attached to various parts of his body, and by dint of a great deal of pulling and hauling, we extricated the unfortunate infant from his awkward position.

The poor little animal had not had a long life before experiencing its ups and downs, and it now looked excessively bewildered at not finding its mother, who had escaped with the rest of the herd. He was soon consoled, however, by being allotted to a tame matron, who did not seem particularly pleased at being thus installed in the office of foster mother whether she liked it or not.

We now all jogged home in great spirits, and, though Jung professed himself dissatisfied with only having captured four out of a herd of twelve, we were perfectly contented with a day's work which my elephant-shooting experience in Ceylon had never seen equalled, and which so fully realised the promise made by the Minister at starting, that we should be the first to partake of a sport to be met with only in the noble forests of his native country.

CHAPTER VI.

March to Bhimphede—National defences—The Cheesapany pass—Lovely scenery—Night adventure—The watch-fire—Reception at camp—Arrival at Katmandu.

We had looked forward with no little anxiety to the morning following our elephant-hunt, as we were to go in search of rhinoceros : it was therefore a severe disappointment to us when Jung entered our tent at daylight, and informed us that it was necessary we should at once proceed on our way to Katmandu. The reason he gave us was, that we should have to go too far out of our route before we could find our game : however that might be, there was no help for it, and we commenced our march up the valley of the Rapti, along the narrow rocky path leading to Bhimphede, our next halting-place. It was a five hours' march, and we crossed the river thirty-two times before we came in sight of the picturesque Durumsolah, or native rest-house, which is situated at the head of the valley. Hills clothed to their summits with variegated jungle rose above us to an immense but not uniform height, and the scenery looked bolder as we became more enclosed among the mountains.

Bhimphede is a Newar village, the inhabitants

being the aborigines of the country. It is said to derive its name from a Hindoo divinity named Bheem having on some occasion happened to stop there. It is distant from Hetowra about 18 miles, and the road might be much improved by a little engineering.

The present policy of the Nepaul government is to keep the roads by which their country is approached in as impassable a state as possible, vainly imagining that, in case of a war, the badness of the roads would offer an insuperable obstacle to our progress, and compel us to relinquish any attempt to penetrate to Katmandu. This delusion ought to have been dispelled by the occupation of Muckwanpore by Sir David Ochterlony; not that it is a contingency they need take much trouble to provide against, since it would never be worth our while to do more than take possession of the Terai.

The present state of the roads renders it impossible for goods to be conveyed into Nepaul, except upon men's backs; and as the traffic would be considerable in various articles of commerce, the prosperity and wealth of the country would be incalculably increased by an improvement in the means of transit.

Jung Bahadoor is quite alive to the real state of the case, and sees at once the absurdity of the policy pursued by the Nepaul government, but he feels that any innovation of the sort would be too unpopular for him to attempt in his present position. His recently imbibed liberal notions coincide but little with the cramped ideas of a semi-barbarous durbar. He is well aware that neither bad roads, troops, nor any other obstacle that he could oppose to our advance, would avail in case of our invading Nepaul. His feeling as regards a war with the British was not inaptly expressed in a remark he once made to me,—" If a cat is pushed into a corner it will fly at an elephant, but it will always try to keep out of the corner as long as possible."

At Bhimphede, where we arrived about midday, I dismounted from the elephant on which I had journeyed comfortably for 200 miles, and for which I had begun to feel quite an affection, and was soon high up the precipitous ascent of the Cheesapany pass. It crosses a mountain which rises nearly 2000 feet above the village at its base; the path is so steep that a horse can barely scramble up it; and the ascent of the Rigi, in Switzerland, seemed a mere nothing in comparison; this pass in its turn is not nearly so steep as the Chandernagiri, which is the last pass before you descend into the valley of Katmandu.

Having so much mountain work before me, I determined on walking the rest of the journey, that being the most satisfactory and enjoyable way of travelling across a highland country and viewing its scenery; my companion betook himself to a cot or dandy swung on a pole, preferring that method of getting carried over the hills to the one in general use amongst the natives, which I imagine is peculiar to Nepaul. An open-mouthed conical-basket, like that of the Parisian chiffonnier, but with contents in some respects different, since this contains the traveller and not the shreds of his exploded journal, is fastened upon the back of a bearer by a strap across his forehead and two others over his shoulders; the occupant sits with his legs over the rim of the basket, and his back almost resting against the head of his bearer, who, bending forward under the weight of his load, and grasping a long stick, looks like some decrepit old man—a delusion which vanishes the instant you commence the ascent of a mountain by his side, when his endurance and vigor astonish you, if they do not knock you up.

Before we had toiled half way up the precipitous ascent, the view, that great alleviator of fatigue to the mountain traveller, was suddenly hidden from us by a thick mist in which we became enveloped, and which, rolling slowly over the hills, hid from our gaze a magnificent panorama of the lovely valley along which our morning's march had led us, and which lay stretched at our feet. With its broad stream winding down its centre, it reminded me of many similar valleys in Switzerland and the Tyrol, more particularly the Engadine, as seen from the hill above Nauders : while the hills, richly clad with masses of dark foliage, and rising to a height of two or three thousand feet, more nearly resembled those of the Cinnamon Isle. There is a fort near the summit of the pass with a few hundred soldiers, and a sort of custom-house, at which two sentries are placed for the purpose of levying a tax amounting to about sixpence upon every bundle passing either in or out of the Nepaul dominions ; whether it be a bundle of grass or a bale of the valuable fabric manufactured from the shawl-goat of Thibet, the same charge is made, rendering it a grievously heavy tax upon the poor man with his load of wood, while it is a matter of no importance to the rich merchant whose coolies are freighted with rare and valuable merchandize.

Having accomplished nearly half the descent of the opposite side, we emerged from the mist, and a view of a wilder valley opened up, in which the streams were more rapid and furious, and the mountains which enclosed it more rugged and precipitous. A few trees, principally firs, were here and there scattered over the bare face of the mountain wherever they could find a sufficiently-sheltered nook. Enterprising settlers had perched themselves upon the naked shoulders of the hills, or were more snugly ensconced below by the side of the brawling stream, which was crossed here and there by primitive bridges, consisting of a log or two thrown from one heap of stones to another, with a few turfs laid upon them.

I observed in the Nepaul valleys—what must be the case in every country in which the hills are composed of a soft material—deltas formed by the soil which is washed down by the mountain torrents. The mass of débris in the valley often extends quite across it, and forces the stream through a gorge, frequently of considerable grandeur in those places where the power of the torrent during the rains is very great.

This circumstance adds greatly to the beauty of the scenery in the Tyrol, where the limestone formation of the hills thus worked upon spreads a soil in swelling knolls over the valley, on which the most luxuriant vineyards are picturesquely terraced. The effect, however, is very different in Nepaul, where the hills are composed chiefly of gravel and conglomerate ; the deltas, consequently, produce crops of stones more frequently than of anything else. Notwithstanding the want of cultivation in the valley on which we were now looking down, it was full of a sublime beauty, the mountains at either end towering to a height of three or four thousand feet, while the path we were to follow was to be seen on the opposite side, winding over a formidable range, and always appearing to mount the steepest hills and to go down unnecessarily into innumerable valleys. It was with no little regret then that we made the almost interminable descent, apparently for the mere purpose of starting fair from the bottom of the valley, before we commenced the arduous climb in store for us over a range still higher than the one we had just traversed.

We crossed the stream at the bottom by a single-arched bridge of curious mechanism and peculiar to the Himalayas, the chief advantage being the large span, which admits of an immense body of water rushing through; a necessary precaution in the case of a mountain torrent. We then toiled up the hill side by a fearfully narrow path. At times my companion seemed absolutely hanging over the precipice; and our path was not in some places above twelve inches broad; had we slipped we must inevitably have become food for the fishes in the Pomonia, which was gliding rapidly along some hundreds of feet below, and which we were informed was a good trouting stream.

At last we reached the summit of the range, from which we had a lovely view of the surrounding country; the hills were just tipped by the setting sun; but this fact, while it added to the beauty of the scene, materially detracted from our enjoyment of it. In a few moments more we should be benighted, and we ha l still two hours' walk to tho village for which we were bound. Accordingly, we had scarcely commenced the descent when it became so dark that it was no longer possible to distinguish the path; and having a vivid recollection of the precipices I had already passed, I felt no inclination to risk a fall of a few hundred feet. After making some little progress by feeling our way with sticks, we found it hopeless, and fairly gave in, having no alternative but to make the narrow path we were on our resting-place for the remainder of the night. This was a most disagreeable prospect, and we regretted that we had allowed Jung and his suite to ride on. The minister had recommended us to follow in cots, as he thought the road was too bad for men accustomed to level country to ride along. It was vain to tell him that we could ride where he could, or that we had seen hills before we came to Nepaul; he insisted that he was responsible for our safety, and would not hear of our riding. As we had little anticipated so arduous a march at starting, we had not thought it worth while further to contest the point with one who knew the country so well; and now, when it was too late, we sincerely wished ourselves comfortably lodged in his camp.

I had already walked for six consecutive hours over roads exceeding in danger and difficulty most of the mountain passes in Switzerland, and began to feel fatigued and not a little hungry, seeing that I had not touched a morsel of food since daybreak, with the exception of a crust of bread that I had found in my pocket.

Thus the prospect of stretching myself out on a slippery path, with a stone for my pillow, and the contemplation of my miseries for my supper, was anything but agreeable.

As we were in this humour it was not to be wondered at that an intelligent soldier, whom we had for a guide, came in for a certain amount of our indignation when he informed us that it was still four coss (eight miles) to Pheer Phing, the place to which we were bound. Base deceiver!—he had told us at starting that it was not quite four coss, and now, after walking hard for six hours, we had got rather farther from it than we were at starting. It was impossible, at this rate, to say when our journey would come to an end. Nor could we get him to admit his error, and own that one or other of his statements must be wrong. He was a good-hearted fellow withal, and bore us no malice for our ill temper, but gave me a walking-stick and an orange as peace-offerings. However, he rigidly maintained his assertion as to the distance, at the same time suggesting that we should push on, encouraging us with the assurance that the rest of the path was a maidan or dead level. As he had made a similar statement at starting, and as the only bit of level walking we could remember was a log bridge, over which we had crossed, we knew too well what amount of confidence to put in this assertion.

At last one of the bearers who had gone on to

explore the path ahead came back with the animating intelligence "that he saw a fire." We therefore determined to make for it with all diligence, and soon perceived the bright glare of a large watch-fire, with a party of soldiers crowded round it. We gladly joined them, and while one of their number was sent forward for torches we rolled ourselves in our cloaks near the crackling blaze, for the night was bitterly cold ; and, heaping up fresh logs upon the fire, a bright flame lit up the wild scene.

We forgot our miseries as we watched the picturesque group of weather-beaten Ghorkas, or gathered what we could from their conversation, of their opinions upon the politics of the country, and the trip of the prime minister, on both which subjects they expressed themselves pretty freely, and took pains to impress upon us how anxious they were for our safe arrival in camp, informing us that their heads would be the price of any accident that should happen to us. At last the torches were seen flickering on the opposite hill, and soon afterwards we commenced our march in picturesque procession, passing over rugged ascents, across brawling rocky streams, and down dark romantic glens, until we began to think that the existence of Pheer Phing was a fiction.

It was about nine o'clock when I perceived we had entered a town which, by its brick pavement and high houses, I concluded to be a large one. After crossing three ranges of mountains, each nearly two thousand feet high, we did not much speculate upon anything but the distance still to be travelled; and the numerous lights twinkling in the distance were a welcome evidence of the proximity of Jung's encampment. The minister came out and received us cordially, expressing his regret at our misadventure and the anxiety he had been in as to our fate; for the route we had taken was not the ordinary one, but one of those short cuts which so often prove the unwary traveller's greatest misfortune. As our servants had not yet come up, he insisted upon our partaking of the repast he had prepared for us. I did not require a second invitation, and all scruples vanished as I looked with delight at the little leaf cups containing the scented greasy condiments formerly despised, and unhesitatingly plunged my fingers (for of course there were no spoons or forks) into a mass of rice and mixed it incontinently with everything within reach, disregarding the Jung's remonstrances, that this was salt-fish and the other sweetmeat, and that they would not be good together. After fasting for fifteen hours, and being in hard exercise the greater part of that time, one is not disposed to be particular, and to this day I have not the slightest conception what I devoured for the first ten minutes; at the end of that time my first sensation was peculiarly disagreeable—namely, that my hunger was sufficiently appeased to allow me to consider what I was eating ; at this point I stopped, still rather hungry, but better off than my companion, who, having retained his presence of mind, had not touched anything.

We now got into palanquins prepared for us, and arrived at the residency at Katmandu at three in the morning, in a comatose state, arising partly from fatigue, partly from drowsiness, but chiefly, I imagine, from peculiar feeding.

CHAPTER VII.

The British residency—Houses at the temple of Pusputnath—Unprepossessing appearance of the Newar population—Their dress and characteristic features—Ghorkas—Temple of Pusputnath—View from the hill above it—The temple of Bhood—Worshippers from Thibet and Chinese Tartary—Their singular and disgusting appearance—Striking scene in the grand square of the city of Katmandu.

I DID not awake until the day was far advanced, and my first impulse was to look out of my window, with no little curiosity, expecting to see the Snowy Range somewhere in the heavens near the sun ; in this I was disappointed, for the mist was so dense that neither sun nor Snowy Range was visible ; we therefore determined to go in search of less exalted objects of interest.

But ere we canter away from the door of the residency upon the shaggy little ponies which had been provided for our use by the Durbar, the Company's establishment in Nepaul demands a moment's attention. In the only thoroughly independent state extant in India the British Government is represented by a Resident, to whose hospitality we were much indebted during our delightful stay in Katmandu. His house, a Gothic mansion of a rather gingerbread appearance, is situated in a well laid-out park-like enclosure, which forms the residency grounds, and which contains two or three neat substantial houses, the habitations of the two officers of the embassy. One of them kindly accompanied us in our search after sights, and directed our steps in the first instance to the temple of Pusputnath. We passed through the suburbs of Katmandu by a road beautifully paved, in some places with brick, in others with granite. It was along this road that the body of Martibar Singh, the late prime minister, and uncle of Jung Bahadoor, was dragged after he had been shot by his nephew, and was burned on the bank of the Bhagmutty before the soldiery (with whom he was an especial favourite) had any idea of his having been killed.

As I approached the temple I remarked some handsome houses, three or four stories in height, which we were informed were the residences of some of the priests. As they were good specimens of the architecture of this country, I may as well describe them here.

The whole front of the Nepaulese houses presented a mass of curiously carved wood-work, so that the beautiful flat brick of which they were built (and for the manufacture of which Nepaul is famous) was scarcely discernible amidst the intricate tracery which surrounded every window, and hung in broad wooden fringes from the balconies: these are formed under the eaves, which project five or six feet, and are supported by rafters, on which quaint figures are depicted in all sorts of impossible postures; the space between the rafters is also filled by carved wood, forming a sort of balcony or small room, generally occupied by the women of the establishment, and flat faces peer out of grotesque windows as you pass beneath.

But it must not be imagined that the same attraction exists here as in other Oriental countries to induce you to return their gaze. On the contrary, the female portion of the Nepaulese community is anything but attractive. I have seldom seen a race look more debased and squalid. Sometimes a florid tint about the nose and cheek-bones seems to hint at an affection for the bottle; while their flowing or rather tangled locks, and slovenly dress, might fairly induce the suspicion that they had but lately parted company with it. The Newar women, however, were ladylike in their appearance, when compared with some of the Bootya tribe with whom I afterwards made acquaintance.

It would, perhaps, be hardly fair to these copper-coloured ladies to judge entirely from their appearance, but, from what I could learn, it did not belie them, except, of course, as regards their friendship for the bottle, drunkenness being a vice which is not prevalent, though the strictness with respect to intoxicating liquors, so remarkable amongst the Hindoos of the plains, is by no means observable among the hill tribes.

The dress of the men consists of a short coat, not unlike a shooting-coat, reaching about half-way to the knees, and composed of a coarse cotton fabric manufactured in the country, from a tree which is a native of some of the lower valleys, but which I did not see in the valley of Katmandu.

In the colder months they wear home-spun woollen clothes. The dress of the women differs little from that of the men, except that the coat is longer, resembling a dressing-gown, and a sort of bodice is generally worn beneath it; a white shawl wrapped round the waist completes one of the most ungraceful costumes imaginable. All the men and some of the women are armed with the kukri, a heavy-bladed weapon or knife of singular shape. But lest this be too unprepossessing a picture of the Newars, or aborigines of Nepaul (for the Ghorkas are a superior and very different race), I should remark that I had no opportunity of seeing any of the females of the higher orders of either nation. The Ghorkas, being, for the most part, bigoted Hindoos, are prevented by their religion from allowing the women to appear in public. The Newars, not fettered by any such restraint, can now boast very few noble families; the ancient grandees of the Newar dynasty are extirpated, with the exception of one or two of the old aristocracy, who are in the last stage of decay. I cannot agree with Colonel Kirkpatrick (who wrote an account of his visit to Nepaul in 1803) in thinking that, "though the Newars have round and rather flat faces, small eyes and low spreading noses, they bear no resemblance to Chinese features;" on the contrary, I was much struck with the great similarity of the mass of the lower orders to the Chinese. Their imperturbable good humour and unaffected simplicity as plainly proved them a hill race, as did their picturesque dwellings and sturdy limbs. Altogether this class of the inhabitants of Nepaul are a cheerful, happy race, for whom one could feel a sort of affection after becoming reconciled to their appearance; but a woman is certainly not fascinating when what ought to be nose is nothing but cheek with two holes in it, and what ought to be neck is almost body as well. If people have protuberances in wrong places, it of course requires a little time for the eye to become accustomed to them. It may be that a goître is a beauty in the eyes of many a young Nepaulese swain. It matters little, however, to a young Newar bride whether her husband admires her or not, for she is at liberty to claim a divorce whenever she pleases, and, if her second choice be not of lower caste than herself, she may leave him at pleasure and return to her original spouse, resuming the charge of any family she may have had by him.

The Ghorkas are the conquerors of Nepaul, and now compose the army; they have grants of land called jaghires, on which they live when not actually on service. They are a handsome and independent race, priding themselves upon not being able to do anything but fight; and in their free and sometimes noble carriage often reminded me of the Tyrolese.

Besides the Ghorkas and Newars there are two or three other tribes, each consisting of but a limited number, and possessing no peculiar distinguishing marks, except the differences to be found in their religious opinions, which are generally a mixture of the Bhuddist and Hindoo creeds.

But to return to the temple of Pusputnath. This celebrated edifice is said to have been erected by Pussoopush Deoth, the fourth prince of the Soorijbunsee dynasty; and so sacred is the temple considered, that a pilgrimage to its shrines is held to be more meritorious than any other act that can be performed by a Hindoo. As the massive folding-doors opened before us, the view of the court-yard was certainly more striking than anything I had yet seen of the sort. Immediately opposite the handsome gateway, and situated in the centre of the court-yard, was the temple, roofed with lead, while the edges were ornamented with a profusion of gold leaf. Beside the large doors of massive silver were finely carved windows, covered in all directions with devices in the same precious metal.

Four sculptured lions guarded the double flight of steps, while at the bottom of the principal flight was a large figure of a kneeling bull (nanda), executed in copper, and superbly gilt. The rest of the court-yard was filled with images and shrines of various descriptions ; a kneeling figure of Siva, a huge bell, more lions, and other sacred objects being studded throughout it in odd confusion. After looking at the varied and somewhat brilliant objects about us, our attention was directed to the roof of the temple, and certainly the transition from the sublime to the ridiculous was extraordinary. Pots, pans, old kukris, dusty-looking musical instruments, goods and chattels of all descriptions, such as one might imagine would form the contents of a Nepaulese pawnbroker's shop, if there is any such establishment here, were wedged together indiscriminately beneath the projecting roof of the pagoda, for of that Chinese form was this much venerated *Hindoo* temple. This mass of incongruous wares, as far as I could learn, was composed of the unclaimed goods of pious worshippers, persons dying without known heirs, and certainly, to judge from their appearance, the heirs did not lose much by not establishing their claims.

We ascended the hill, immediately under which the temple is situated, and were charmed with the lovely prospect which it commanded. On the left, and clothing with its brilliant colours a gentle slope, was the grove sacred to Siva, divided by the equally sacred Bhagmutty from the temple we had just visited, and into which we now looked down. The Bhagmutty was crossed by two narrow Chinese-looking bridges, resembling those we have such frequent opportunities of admiring on the willow-pattern plates. It is at this sacred spot that devout Hindoos wish to die, with their feet in the water. Here it is that the bodies of the great are burnt; Martibar Singh was reduced to ashes at the end of the bridge, and so was the Ranee not three months before my visit, together with two favourite female slaves, whose society she did not wish to relinquish.

Beyond this interesting foreground stretched the luxuriant valley, its gentle slopes and eminences terraced to their summits, which were often crowned by some old fortified Newar town: the terraces, tinged with the brilliant green of the young crops, rose one above another to the base of the walls, while beneath the Bhagmutty wound its tortuous course to the romantic gorge in the mountains, through which it leaves this favoured valley to traverse lazily the uninteresting plains of upper India.

A peak of the gigantic Himaleh, bursting through the bank of clouds which had hitherto obscured it, reared its snow-capped summit far up towards the skies, and completed this noble prospect.

Crossing the river, we proceeded to visit the temple sacred to Bhood, the resort of the numerous tribes of Bhootiyas, or inhabitants of the highlands of Thibet and Chinese Tartary, who perform annual pilgrimages hither in the winter, but are obliged to return to their homes early in the spring, being unable to endure the heat of a Nepaulese summer.

This remarkable building was visible some time before we reached it, and is of the form peculiar to Bhuddist places of worship in other parts of the world, but more particularly in Anuradhupoora and the ancient cities of Ceylon, the ruins of which bear testimony to the existence of larger Dagobas than that before which the followers of the Buddhist faith worship in the valley of Katmandu.

The pyramidal summit was gorgeously gilt, and terminated in a huge bell adorned in the same glittering manner, producing a brilliant effect as it brightly reflected the rays of the noonday sun. The massive stone platform on which the Dagoba stood was square; the ascent to it on each side was by a broad flight of steps; but on the lower part of the pyramid, staring Chinese-looking eyes, painted in brilliant colours, detracted considerably from the imposing effect which a massive pile of stone and brick, not less than 120 feet high, would otherwise have produced.

We rode round it in a sort of court-yard,

enclosed by small two-storied houses, which were very filthy, and out of which emerged men, women, and children, very filthy also; we were soon encompassed by a crowd of the most disreputable, dissolute-looking wretches imaginable. The women were dressed in thick woollen gowns, which had once been red, and reached a little below the knee; these were loosely fastened round the waist, remaining open or closed above, as the case might be. The children, notwithstanding the inclement temperature, were in the cool and airy costume common to the rising generation in the East. The men were dressed exactly like the women, their matted hair and beard, flat noses, and wide eyes, generally bloodshot, giving them a disgusting appearance. Both sexes wore a sort of woollen gaiter, open at the calf, the protruding muscle of which looked as if nothing could have confined it; their shoes, as far as the dust would allow me to see, were of the same material. They seemed good-natured and inoffensive, but are not free from the vice of drunkenness; they consume quantities of tea prepared with rancid lard.

Had I been asked to determine the origin of this race, I should have pronounced it to be a mixture of Naples lazzaroni with the scum of an Irish regiment. The ruddy complexions of some of the women, and the swarthy look of many of the men, might fairly warrant such a conclusion. They were so importunate and offensive as they pressed round me that I hurried over my sketch of the temple, and made my escape from them, not, however, without once more looking round with interest on the crowd of beings whose distant habitations were upon the northern slope of the Himalayan chain, hitherto unvisited by any European, except Dr. Hooker, and consequently almost totally unknown.

I quite envied them the journey they were about to undertake, which would occupy them three weeks; the large droves of sheep by which they are always accompanied carried their limited worldly possessions, together with the various tokens of civilization which they had procured in the (to them) highly civilized country they were now visiting, and on which no doubt their Bhootan friends would look with no little awe and wonderment.

This wandering and singular race do not visit Nepaul solely to worship at the temple of Bhood, but have an eye to business as well as religion. I shall have occasion by and by to speak of the numerous articles which they import into Nepaul on the backs of sheep, over the rocky passes which lead from the cold region they inhabit.

On our way from the temple of Bhood, which, by the by, had just been furbished up and whitewashed by a great man from H'Lassa, an emissary of the Grand Lama's, we passed through the town of Katmandu, which was entered by a massive gateway, the city being surrounded by a wall. Long narrow streets, very fairly paved, lead in all directions; the houses are not so high as those of Benares or Cairo; the streets are broader, and some of them would admit of the passage of a carriage. They are all well drained and comparatively clean, contrasting most favourably in that respect with any other Oriental town I have ever seen. The streets were filled with foot-passengers, in bright and variegated costumes, passing busily on, or stopping to make purchases at the shops, which were on the ground-floor, with the whole front open, and the merchant sitting in the midst of his wares. The next story is inhabited, I believe, by his family; but I did not gain an entrance into any of the common houses. The outside front generally presented a mass of wood carving, each small window surrounded by a border two or three feet broad, while under the eaves of the house projected the singular balcony I have already described.

The great square, in which is situated the Durbar, or palace of the King, presented in itself almost all the characteristic features of a Nepaul town. As it suddenly burst upon us on turning the corner of the long street leading from the city-gate, the view was in every respect most striking. This square, or court, is well paved, and contains the Chinese pagoda, composed entirely of wood, from which it is said the town derives its name. Its three or four roofs, glittering one above another, are supported by grotesque representations of unknown deities, and figures of all sizes and colors, not always of the most proper description. The whole formed a mass of green, gold leaf, and vermilion ; and was guarded by a sentry, who, in order to be in keeping with his charge, wore a long flowing gown of bright colors, reaching to his ankles, and marched backwards and forwards at the top of a long flight of steps. A couple of well-carved lions, in grey sandstone, guarded the lower steps as efficiently as he did the upper ones. There were at least four pagodas, painted in like way, and guarded in like manner, in the great square of Katmandu. The guard-house contained a large stand of arms of antique construction. There was also the Durbar, the residence of the Rajah, a straggling building, almost European in its style, and gaudy enough to please even the late King of Bavaria ; close to it was a huge deformed image of Siva, sitting in an uncomfortable posture on a square stone, violently gesticulating with her fourteen arms, perhaps at a party of heretical Bhootyas who were passing tranquilly by, leading along their sheep, decidedly the cleanest and most respectable-looking members of the group. Beyond, high and gloomy houses almost touched, their wooden fringes creaking responsively to one another across the narrow streets, while the owners of the cobwebby tenements, peeping out of the narrow windows in their balconies, made their remarks upon the strangers in not much more melodious tones ; in an old court-yard a little way above, was visible an unwieldy rhinoceros, placidly contemplating a bundle of grass, from which it had satisfied its hunger, in happy ignorance that its life is dependent on that of the Rajah ; for in Nepaul it is a rule that the death of one great animal should be immediately followed by that of another, and, when a Rajah dies, a rhinoceros is forthwith killed to keep him company. As he stood tethered almost under the palace windows, we thought him at once a fitting moral and a characteristic background to this novel and interesting picture.

CHAPTER VIII.

The Temple of Sumboonath—View from the platform of the temple—The valley of Nepaul and its resources—Tradition respecting it—Entrance of the Prime Minister into Katmandu—The two kings—A brilliant reception.

THE temple of Sumboonath, which we next visited, is situated on the summit of a woody eminence; it is approached by a long flight of steps, the trouble of ascending which is amply compensated by the lovely view which the platform of the temple commands, as well as by an inspection of the curious construction of the building itself.

Sumboonath is looked upon as one of the oldest temples in Nepaul, and was erected, according to Kirkpatrick, when Nepaul was ruled by a race of Thibetians; its possession was at one time claimed by the Dalai Lama, or Sovereign Pontiff of H'Lassa, but he has since been obliged to abandon the claim.

The Dagoba resembles the temple of Bhood, but is only about half its size; the spire is covered with plates of copper, gilt. It is surrounded by pagodâs, as well as numerous more modern shrines of a bastard Hindoo class, to which Bhootyas and Bhamas, a tribe of Newars, resort in great numbers. Occasionally the Ghorkas visit these shrines; the thunderbolt of Indra, which is here exhibited, being, I suppose, the object of attraction to them, as they pride themselves on being orthodox Hindoos.

This collection of temples is surrounded by rickety old houses, inhabited by Bhootyas and priests. All around small images sit upon wet stones, holding in their hands everlasting tapers, and look out of their niches upon the dirty worshippers who smother them with faded flowers. Turning our backs upon these little divinities, we obtained the first panoramic view we had yet had of the valley and city of Katmandu.

The valley is of an oval shape; its circumference is nearly 50 miles, and the hills by which it is enclosed vary from one to two thousand feet in height. Sheopoorie, the most lofty of these, is clothed to the summit with evergreen jungle, and rises abruptly behind the town. Behind it the fantastically shaped Jib Jibia shows its craggy summit thickly powdered with snow, while the still loftier Gosian-Thān, at a distance of about 30 miles, rears its ever white and glittering peak to a height of 25,000 feet, and seems majestically to preside over this glorious scene.

The town of Katmandu, situated at the junction of the Bhagmutty and Bishmutty, and containing a population of 50,000 inhabitants, lay spread at our feet, and we could discern the passengers on the narrow fragile-looking bridges which span the two rivers, at this time containing scarcely any water. Innumerable temples, Bhuddist and Hindoo, and mixtures of both, occupied hillocks, or were situated near the sacred fonts or groves with which the valley abounds, and which adds much to the beauty of its appearance. The number of the edifices affords strong proof of the superstition of the people, and warrants the remark of Colonel Kirkpatrick, who says that there seem to be in Nepaul as many shrines as houses, and as many idols as inhabitants.

A tradition is current in Nepaul that the valley of Katmandu was at some former period a lake, and it is difficult to say in which character it would have appeared the most beautiful. The knolls, wooded or terraced, with romantic old Newar towns crowning their summits,—the five rivers of the valley winding amongst verdant meadows,—the banks here and there precipitous, where the soft clayey soil had yielded to the action of the torrent in the rains, —the glittering city itself,—the narrow paved ways leading between high hedges of prickly pear,—the pagodas and temples studded in all directions, presented a scene as picturesque and perhaps more interesting than would have been afforded by the still lake embedded in wild mountains, and frowned upon by snow-capped peaks; while the richly cultivated knolls in the valley formed fertile islands, the luxuriant vegetation of which would have softened the scene into one of exquisite beauty.

Whether the rich and wonderfully prolific soil of the valley is the alluvial deposit of this lake, I cannot say, but there is no doubt that, whatever may be the cause, the valley of Nepaul is almost unrivalled in its fertility, supporting as it does in comfort and plenty a population of 400,000 inhabitants, being 300 persons to the square mile.

There is not, I conceive, any other mountainous country in the world that can boast of possessing so favoured a spot. Throughout its whole length and breadth, not a stone is to be found; it is well watered; its temperature is delightful, the thermometer in the hottest month seldom reaches 75°, in the coldest never falls below 30°; it is sufficiently near the tropics to rejoice in the presence of the warm bright sun even in the depth of winter, while the proximity of the ever snow-capped "Himaleh" prevents the heat being too severely felt in the middle of summer. It rarely freezes in the valley, and never snows, although the hills around, some of which do not exceed 1000 feet, are frequently powdered.

It is impossible to conceive a more enjoyable climate, and the numerous productions of which the valley can boast betoken its genial influences.

I am sorry that I cannot from my own observation testify to the rich variety of its vegetable productions, as the time of year during which I was in Nepaul was unfavourable, but many English forest-trees flourish here,—amongst them, oaks, chestnuts, and pines ; rhododendrons also abound, and I observed almost every species of English fruit-tree ; in the residency garden all the European vegetables are raised to perfection.

But to return from this digression on the advantages of soil and climate which the valley possesses. The lovely view before us comprised in a glance the grand and majestic scenery of the mountains, with the softer but still animating view of the luxuriant plain, bearing evidence of that large and industrious population whose habitations were so picturesquely grouped throughout it.

We had not nearly satisfied our desire to gaze upon so much that was new and interesting, when we were informed by our attendants that the astrologers had announced the auspicious moment at which the Minister Sahib, or, as we must now call him, Jung Bahadoor Comaranagee, should leave the camp outside the city walls and make an imposing entry into Katmandu.

This lucky hour was now close at hand ; and as the entrance of the prime minister into the capital was a scene not to be lost, we hurried down to be in time for the ceremony of his reception.

In a few moments we were rattling in one of

the only carriages in Nepaul over one of the only carriage-roads of which it can boast, and soon reached the bridge, near which was pitched a spacious tent. On our way we passed a square lined with soldiers, and the streets were crowded with a motley population, such as it would be vain to endeavour to describe, but which increased in density as we approached the centre of attraction, near which we were obliged to leave the carriage, and were conducted between rows of soldiers by various members of the royal household, each of us being led by the hand in the most affectionate manner. My conductor was a brother of Jung Bahadoor's, who distinguished himself about a week afterwards by a base attempt to assassinate the minister. I was unfortunate in my friends in other instances besides this; one old man, who had accompanied the minister to Europe, and was an especial ally of mine on board ship, was implicated in the same vile plot against the life of the man towards whom he had every reason to feel grati tude, if such a sentiment is known amongst Orientals. Poor old Kurbeer Kutrie was a venerable-looking dignified old man, bigoted to an excess, and thoroughly disgusted with his trip to the land of the beef-eaters, though he could not but admit that what he saw was wonderful! The ignominious punishment which was inflicted upon him for his share in the conspiracy, and by which he lost caste, was doubtless more severely felt by him than death would have been. Not that it signifies in the least in Nepaul whether a man is a fratricide or prefers making away with more distant relatives. If you do not associate with assassins, you must give up the pleasures of Nepaul society. Among the natives assassination is not looked upon as a crime, but as a matter of course; the minister, however, with those of his suite who accompanied him on his recent mission, have become more enlightened in this respect, and have found to their astonishment that indiscriminate murder is not the usual mode adopted in the civilized world for bringing about political changes or accomplishing private ends.

Jung Bahadoor, no doubt, now wishes that more of the Durbar had made the same trip, and profited by it in like manner, since the custom above alluded to must be highly inconvenient to him, more particularly since he has eight brothers, most of whom cast a longing eye towards the premiership; a man's chance of filling this office not depending upon his power "to form a ministry," so much as upon his accuracy in taking aim and his skill in seizing any opportunity offered by his rival of showing his dexterity in a manner more personal than pleasant. Jung Bahadoor may well exclaim, "Save me from my brothers!" Already has one of them attempted his life; but the Minister has learned mercy in England, and, to the astonishment of every one,

Budreenath Sing and his fellow conspirators are only banished for life. It is said that the minister resisted all the representations of his friends as to the propriety of executing the conspirators by the argument of "What would the 'Times' say?"—which must have appeared to the majority of the members of the Nepaul Durbar to be a very extraordinary reason for leniency.

Bum Bahadoor had acted as prime minister during the absence of his brother in England, and had just learned to value the possession of power when the return of the minister put an end to his short-lived greatness, and he would have sunk at once into comparative insignificance, had not Jung, who knew enough of human nature to guess the sentiments of a man in such a position, judiciously gilded the pill by making him Commander-in-Chief of the Forces.

Grasping the friendly hand of my conductor, in happy ignorance of his fratricidal intentions, I followed immediately behind the minister, whose return to Nepaul, after he had encountered the perils of land and sea, and paid a visit to the Queen of the greatest country in the world, not even excepting China, was a matter of so much importance, that the Rajah himself came from his palace to the spot where we were now assembled, to meet one who had been favoured with an interview with so mighty a monarch, and who had in his possession the letter from her majesty of England to his majesty of Nepaul. We were, therefore, prepared to see the king seated on a divan, and arrayed in gorgeous attire; but who the old gentleman was who was sitting with most perfect sang froid next him on his elevated seat, I was at a loss to conceive. Whoever he was, he seemed most perfectly at home, and I found on inquiry it was natural he should be so, for the old man was sitting on his own throne, which had been usurped by his son, he having been dethroned on the score of imbecility. Such being the case, why he was allowed to occupy the place he did was inexplicable, unless it were to prove that he really was unfit to sit upon the throne alone, since he was content to share it upon grand occasions with his son, whenever this latter precocious young gentleman, who was, as it were, the representative of "Young Nepaul," chose to give his venerable father a treat.

But it would be useless to speculate on the cause of this proceeding, since it is impossible ever to understand, and hopeless to attempt to discover, the motives or secret springs which actuate a native Durbar; and no doubt Jung himself, who is the real manager of everything, had some good reason for the present double occupancy of the throne. It struck me that it would answer one purpose at any rate: it would show the people that the young king looked as imbecile as the old one, while his countenance was far less prepossessing, as he seemed only to have just sense enough to be able to gratify the brutal and sensual passions to which he is a prey; whether the stories of wholesale executions of slaves taking place in his court-yard merely for his amusement are true or not, I cannot say, but he looked capable of any wickedness, and, though not more than twenty-two or twenty-three years old, had already rivalled the atrocities of Nero. His countenance was not unlike those depicted on the walls of Indian towns, with the same large staring eyes, thin twisted moustache, sensual lips, and thick bull neck. His dress was handsome, and his jewels were magnificent; but in dress, in carriage, and in dignity of manner, the prime minister was unquestionably the most distinguished looking man in Durbar. He wore a magnificent robe of white silk embroidered with gold, and tight pantaloons of rich brocade, which set off his slim figure to advantage; his turban was a mass of sparkling diamonds, and his whole person seemed loaded with jewels. His sturdy body-guard, all armed with double-barrelled rifles, stood close behind his chair, and were the only soldiers in the tent; the nonchalant way in which he addressed the rajah, with folded arms and unbended knee, betokened the unbounded power he possesses in the state. Perhaps it is not very politic in him to arrogate so much to himself in a land where every man's hand is against him, in proportion as he is feared by every one from his majesty downwards.

On each side of the tent stood a row of grandees of the realm, amongst whom the eight brothers of Jung Bahadoor held conspicuous places, while kazies and sirdars continued the line, until they were lost in the crowd of minor officers.

The blaze of jewels, and the glitter of gold and silver, were calculated to strike an European spectator with astonishment, and he might well be startled at so magnificent a display in a highland court.

I observed a few English and French uniforms, covered with a great deal more of gold and silver lace than they were entitled to ; all which gaudy array was the more striking to me when I remembered that I had on a plaid shooting-coat and felt hat. I had no opportunity of explaining to his majesty that plaid shooting-coats and felt hats are the court costume in England, but no doubt he thought it all correct. It is, moreover, the prerogative of Englishmen to sit in the presence of Oriental potentates with their hats on, which prevented my secreting my shabby old wide-awake as I had intended.

As I sat next but one to the minister, I was under the immediate protection of the rifles and pistols, which latter implements protruded in a most formidable manner from the belts of the body-guard. As various Nepaulese nobles of doubtful politics sat in front of his Excellency, he felt these gentlemen-at-arms were peculiarly valuable additions to his retinue, as being ready to act either on the offensive or defensive at a moment's notice. Everything, however, went off with the most perfect harmony; a few compliments were exchanged between himself and his sovereign, and the meeting broke up after the usual ceremony of giving and receiving pawn. This consisted in the presentation by both the kings, to every stranger present, of a small pyramidal packet of leaves, which, when opened by the favoured recipient, was found to contain a few other leaves, stuck together by slimy substances, of unpleasant appearance and aromatic odour. Fortunately, you were not compelled to partake of this in the presence of the royal donor, and means were found to dispose of it slily on leaving his majesty's audience-chamber.

As we were driving back to the Residency, it struck me that the history of a man who, at so early an age, had raised himself from being an ensign in the army to the powerful position which the grand display at his reception had just proved him to hold in his own country, would be interesting, if it were possible to gain any information on the subject that could be relied upon. I therefore determined to collect the best that it was in my power to obtain; and the following particulars, gathered partly from himself, and partly from one who has had many opportunities of becoming acquainted with his history, form, I believe, a trustworthy account of a career which, from its tragic nature, is invested with a thrilling interest, while it faithfully portrays the eventful changes usually attending the life of an Oriental statesman.

CHAPTER IX.

Sketch of the career of His Excellency General Jung Bahadoor, Prime Minister of Nepaul.

It will be necessary before commencing an account of the career of Jung Bahadoor to describe the state in which the political affairs of Nepaul were when his ambition and daring prompted him to play so important a part in its government. Cool, courageous, and an adept in all arts of intrigue, he possessed every qualification necessary to render a man successful in the East, where native courts are incessantly torn asunder by rival factions, and scenes of violence and bloodshed are the result of plots and counterplots, as each party becomes for the time predominant, and its leading man assumes the office of Premier, to be soon after deprived of his short-lived greatness by a successful conspiracy of the opposing party. These in their turn share the same fate, the King and country remaining passive spectators of the struggles between the opposing factions. They are indeed uninteresting to the King, for he is only too delighted to get any one to take the cares of government off his shoulders, and considers his prerogative to consist in enjoying himself as much as possible.

They are equally uninteresting to the country, for these violent dissensions do not arise upon questions of policy, in any way affecting its government. Ministerial explanations are never asked for nor given in the East. The power of the prime minister is absolute till he is shot, when it becomes unnecessary to question the expediency of his measures, and the people are only interested to this extent, that, generally speaking, the longer a Premier can maintain his position, by so much is their prosperity increased.

The two rival factions in Nepaul were the Pandees and Thapas, and in the early part of this century the reins of government were held by one of the most enlightened men that ever attained to the position of prime minister. Bheem Singh Thapa has left behind him numerous monuments of his greatness, calculating, like Napoleon, that his fame would last at least as long as they did. For an unusual number of years did this able minister retain the management of affairs. He was ultimately placed in confinement, on the charge of being accessory to the murder of the Rajah's children by poison. His enemies resorted to an ingenious, though cruel device, to rid themselves altogether of so dreaded a rival. Knowing his high spirit and keen sense of honour, they spread the report that the sanctity of his Zenana had been violated by the soldiery, which so exasperated him that he committed suicide, and was found in his cell with his throat cut from ear to ear; this occurred in the year 1839. His property was of course confiscated, and the greater part of his family banished. His successor, Ram Singh Pandee, did not long enjoy his ill-gotten power, for, having been discovered intriguing against the British with the ministers of other native courts, he was removed at the representations of our government. Mahtabar Singh, a nephew of the former prime minister, Bheem Singh Thapa, had meantime ingratiated himself with the Ranee (Queen), and through her influence succeeded in getting himself appointed to the vacant post of premier—when, as was to be expected, his first act was to decapitate his predecessor, and as many of the Pandee's family as possible.

The brother of Mahtabar Singh was a kazi, commanding a portion of the army stationed on the north-west frontier of Nepaul, and the second of his eight sons was Jung Bahadoor, then a subadar, or ensign. The independent spirit which the young man had manifested from a boy led him into frequent scrapes with the old kazi, and he used to escape the punishments which they entailed by absconding altogether, and remaining absent until he thought his father's wrath had subsided, or until, as was oftener the case, his own resources were expended. These, however, he usually found means to replenish by his expertness at all games of chance with cards and dice, and early in life he became an accomplished gambler. He was moreover a great favourite amongst the soldiers, as well from his readiness to join them in any wild scheme, as from his skill in all manly exercises and accomplishments. At last the young officer, impatient of being under command, decided upon a bolder step than a mere temporary absence without leave, and thinking, no doubt, that it was a duty he owed to society to improve himself as much as possible by seeing the world, he walked across the Nepaul frontier into Upper India, and profitably employed his time by turning his powers of observation to account, thereby gaining considerable insight into the mode of government and resources of our Indian possessions.

After a time his own resources became so greatly diminished that he was obliged to return, trusting to his powers of acting the repentant prodigal to avert the torrent of his father's wrath. The breach of discipline which he had committed was as readily overlooked in Nepaul as it would have been in other more civilised countries, when the offender has good interest to back him; and promotion to the command of a company was given him as the reward of his services while ensign. About this period Jung Bahadoor received the intelligence of the advancement of his uncle, Mahtabar Singh, to the office of prime minister. So fine a chance for an adventurous spirit to push his fortune at court was not to be lost, and once more bidding adieu to the dull out-station at which he was posted, to the constraint of discipline, and to the grumblings of the old martinet, his father, he followed the example of many great men before him, and betook himself to the capital, thinking it the only place in which his talents could be appreciated. Here he possessed frequent opportunities of displaying that aptitude for intrigue to which he mainly owes his present position, coupled as it was with a daring that hesitated not at the performance of any act which his keen perception and subtle understanding pointed out as necessary for the advancement of his own interests. Jung soon after accompanied a secret mission to Benares, to meet one from the northwest, with the view of organising a war against the British. The vigilance of our authorities, however, discovered the existence of this conspiracy, and Jung, together with his compatriots, was ignominiously taken back to his own frontier, and there liberated. On his return to the capital he led much the same life as before, dabbling not a little in politics; and the ambitious views which now began to actuate him rendered him obnoxious to the young prince, then a mere boy of eighteen, who, nevertheless, seemed to share with his father a portion of the executive. Indeed it was difficult to say in whom the sovereign authority rested: for the Ranee, or wife of the old King, had, with the assistance of Mahtabar

Singh, the prime minister, gained a great influence over the mind of the monarch, who seems to have become nearly imbecile.

It was perhaps the near relationship of Jung to the prime minister that brought upon him the ill-will of the Prince, who treated him with the most unmitigated animosity, and used every means in his power surreptitiously to destroy him. On one occasion he ordered him to cross a flooded mountain torrent on horseback, and when he had reached the middle of the current, which was so furiously rapid that his horse could with difficulty keep his footing, the young Prince suddenly called him back, hoping that, in the act of turning, the force of the stream would overpower both horse and rider. This danger Jung escaped, owing to his great nerve and presence of mind. In relating this anecdote he seemed to think that his life had been in more imminent peril than on any other occasion; though the following struck me as being a much more hazardous exploit. After the affair of the torrent the Prince was no longer at any pains to conceal his designs upon the life of the young adventurer, and that life being of no particular value to any one but Jung himself, it was a matter of perfect indifference to anybody and everybody whether the Prince amused himself by sacrificing Jung to his own dislikes or not. It is by no means an uncommon mode of execution in Nepaul to throw the unfortunate victim down a well: Jung had often thought that it was entirely the fault of the aforesaid victim if he did not come up again alive and unhurt. In order to prove the matter satisfactorily, and also be prepared for any case of future emergency, he practised the art of jumping down wells, and finally perfected himself therein. When, therefore, he heard that it was the intention of the Prince to throw him down a well, he was in no way dismayed, and only made one last request, in a very desponding tone, which was, that an exception might be made in his favour as regarded the being cast down, and that he might be permitted to throw himself down. This was so reasonable a request that it was at once granted; and, surrounded by a large concourse of people—the Prince himself being present by way of a morning's recreation—Jung repaired to the well, where, divesting himself of all superfluous articles of clothing, and looking very much as if he were bidding adieu for ever to the happy valley of Nepaul, he crossed his legs, and, jumping boldly down, was lost to the view of the prince and nobles, a dull splash alone testifying to his arrival at the bottom. Fortunately for Jung there was plenty of water—a fact of which most probably he was well aware—and there were, moreover, many chinks and crannies in the porous stone of which the well was built; so, having learnt his lesson, Jung clung dexterously to the side of the well until midnight, when his friends, who had been previously apprised of the part they were to perform, came and rescued him from his uncomfortable position, and secreted him until affairs took such a turn as rendered it safe for Jung Bahadoor to resuscitate himself. Such was the adventure of the well, which, marvellous as it may appear, was gravely related to me by his Excellency, who would have been very much scandalised if I had doubted it, which of course I did not.

While in a story-telling mood, I may as well relate an account that was given me of the manner in which Jung distinguished himself on one occasion with a musk elephant. The story is interesting, as it was by such daring feats that he won for himself the reputation of being the most undaunted sportsman in Nepaul. The elephant in question had been for some time the terror of the neighbourhood, nor was any one found hardy enough to attempt the capture of the rabid monster. At last, so notorious became his destruction of life and property that Jung heard of it, and at once determined to encounter him. The animal was in the habit of passing along the narrow street of a village in the course of his nocturnal depredations. One night Jung posted himself on the roof of a low outhouse, and, as the huge brute walked under the roof, made a vigorous leap, which landed him on the neck of the elephant, and, in spite of all the efforts of the infuriated animal, there he maintained his position until he succeeded in blindfolding him with a cloth, and in securing him to a tree, amidst the shouts of the populace. Lest this story should seem too improbable to be credited, it may be remarked that a musk elephant is often, as was the case in this instance, a tame one, which at a particular season becomes rabid, and, breaking loose, is the terror of the neighbourhood until recaptured.

During this eventful period in Jung Bahadoor's life, his uncle, Mahtabar Singh, continued to administer the affairs of government with tolerable success ; but the Ranee, to whom he was beholden for the position he occupied, turned the influence she had thus obtained over him to a bad account, and this gallant soldier and popular minister ultimately became distrusted and feared by his own friends, with whom the Ranee was no favourite. This unprincipled woman ill repaid the devotion of her minister, for, on his refusing to comply with her request that he should put to death some of her personal enemies, she became at once his implacable foe, and ruthlessly resolved upon the destruction of her hitherto devoted ally. Thus Mahtabar Singh found himself alienated from and distrusted by his own faction, while he was abandoned by his former patroness, for whose favour he had sacrificed their adherence. The Ranee did not hesitate to apply to this very party for assistance in the furtherance of her nefarious design, and the prime minister was doomed to fall a victim to his own indecision by the hands of his favourite nephew.

One night, about eleven o'clock, a messenger came from the palace to inform him that his services were required by their Majesties—for the Queen had always kept up a semblance of friendship with him. Without the slightest suspicion he repaired to the palace, but scarcely had he ascended the great staircase, and was entering the room in which their Majesties were seated, when the report of a pistol rung through the room; the fatal bullet pierced the heart of the gallant old man, who staggered forward, and fell at the feet of the wretched woman who had been the instigator of the cruel murder.

It is difficult to say what were the motives that prompted Jung Bahadoor to the perpetration of this detestable act, of which he always speaks now in terms of the deepest regret, but asserts that it was an act of necessity, from which there was no escaping. The plea which he invariably uses when referring to the catastrophe is, that either his life or his uncle's must have been sacrificed, and he naturally preferred that it should be the latter. However that may be, the immediate effect was, the formation of a new ministry, in which Jung held office in the capacity of commander-in-chief. The premier, Guggun Singh, was associated with two colleagues. A year had hardly elapsed before Guggun Singh was shot while sitting in his own room. This occurred in the year 1846; a sirdar was taken up on suspicion of having committed this murder, and Abiman Singh, one of the premier's colleagues, was ordered by the Queen to put him to death; as, however, the Rajah would not sanction the execution, Abiman Singh refused to obey the command—a proceeding on his part which seems to have raised a suspicion in the mind of Jung that he had been concerned in the assassination. This suspicion he communicated to Futteh Jung, the other colleague of the late prime minister, suggesting that Abiman Singh and the sirdar already in custody should be forthwith executed, and Futteh Jung installed as prime minister. Futteh Jung, however, refused to accede to so strong a measure; and Jung, who was not of a nature to be thwarted in his plans, determined upon temporarily depriving him of his liberty, in order to enable him to put the design into execution himself.

He had no sooner decided upon his line of conduct than he displayed the utmost resolution in carrying it out. On the same night, and while at the palace, the suspicions which Jung already entertained were confirmed by his observing that Abiman Singh ordered his men to load. It was no time for hesitation. The two colleagues, with many of their adherents, were assembled in the large hall, where the Queen, in a highly-excited state, was insisting upon an immediate disclosure of the murderer of Guggun Singh, who was supposed to have been her paramour. At this moment Jung gave the signal for the seizure of Futteh Jung. The attempt was no sooner made than his son, Karak Bikram Sah, imagining that his father's life was at stake, rushed forward to save him, and seizing a kukri, had already dealt Bum Bahadoor a severe blow, when he was cut down by Dere Shum Shere Bahadoor, then a youth of sixteen or seventeen.

Futteh Jung, vowing vengeance on the murderers of his son, sprang forward to avenge his death, and in another moment Bum Bahadoor, already seriously wounded, would have fallen at his feet, when the report of a rifle rang through the hall, and the timely bullet sped by the hand of Jung Bahadoor laid the gallant father by the side of his no less gallant son.

Thus Jung's *coup d'état* had taken rather a different turn from what he had intended; the die, however, was cast, and everything depended upon his coolness and decision in the trying circumstances in which he was placed. Though he may have felt that his life was in most imminent peril, it is difficult to conceive how any man could attain to such a pitch of cool desperation as to enact the scene which closed this frightful tragedy. There still confronted him fourteen of the nobles whose leader had been slain before their eyes, and who thirsted for vengeance; but the appearance at his side of that faithful body-guard, on whose fidelity the safety of the minister has more than once depended, precluded them from seizing the murderer of their chief. It was but too clear to those unhappy men what was to be the last act of this tragedy. Jung received the rifle from the hand of the man next him, and levelled it at the foremost of the little band. Fourteen times did that fatal report ring through the hall as one by one the rifles were handed to one who would trust no eye but his own, and at each shot another noble lay stretched on the ground. Abiman Singh alone escaped the deadly aim ; he managed to reach the door, but there he was cut almost in two by the sword of Krishn Bahadoor.

Thus, in a few moments, and by his own hand, had Jung rid himself of those whom he most feared. In that one room lay the corpses of the highest nobles of the land, shrouded by the dense smoke still hanging in the confined atmosphere, as if to hide the horrors of a tragedy that would not bear the light of day. The massacre now went on in all parts of the building. One hundred and fifty sirdars perished on that eventful night, and the panic was wide-spread and general. Before day had dawned Jung Bahadoor had been appointed prime minister of Nepaul, and had placed guards over the arsenal, treasury, and palace.

In the morning the troops were all drawn up on parade ; before them were placed, in a ghastly heap, the bodies of their late commanders, to which

Jung pointed, as he assured the army that it would find in him all that it had ever found in them, and he consoled many of the officers in a great measure for the loss they had just sustained by granting them immediate promotion. It seems as easy for a daring adventurer to gain the affections of an army in India as in Europe, and Jung found no difficulty in reconciling his Ghorkas to a change of commanders, and they have ever since professed the greatest devotion to his person.

The utmost caution was now necessary on the part of the new premier, who was obliged still to be on his guard, lest the partizans of those whom he had massacred should succeed in organizing a conspiracy against his life; a sirdar was put to death simply because he had a private audience with the King. Circumstances soon showed that Jung had good reason to feel the insecurity of his position. The two elder Princes, sons of a former Queen, had been for some time in confinement, and the Ranee now attempted to induce Jung to put them to death, in order to secure the throne for one of her own sons. This he positively refused to do, and his refusal brought upon him the wrath of this vindictive woman, whose vengeance had already been so signally wreaked on his uncle by his own instrumentality.

He had not played so prominent a part on that occasion without profiting by the lesson he had learnt; and knowing well the character of the woman with whom he had to deal, he took care to obtain accurate intelligence of all that transpired at court.

Information soon reached him that a plot was formed against his life, and that the post of premier had already been promised to his intended murderer, as a reward for so dangerous a service. Once more the command, which had proved so fatal to Mahtabar Singh, issued from the palace, desiring the immediate attendance of the minister; the messenger was the very man at whose hand Jung was to meet his doom. He had scarcely delivered his treacherous message, when he was struck to the ground by one of the attendants of the prime minister. Jung then proceeded on his way to the palace, where he at once demanded of the Rajah to be dismissed from office, or to be furnished with authority to order the destruction of all the enemies of the heir-apparent. The King could not refuse to grant the authority demanded; and it was no sooner granted than Jung seized and beheaded all the adherents of the conspirator.

As the Ranee herself was the most inveterate enemy of the young Prince, the Rajah's order was at once carried into effect against her, and, to her infinite astonishment, she was informed by Jung that she was to leave Nepaul immediately, accompanied by her two sons. It was of no use to resist the successful young adventurer, whose indomitable courage and good fortune had triumphed over the plots and intrigues of his enemies, and who thus saw himself freed from every obstacle to his quiet possession of the government.

The Rajah accompanied the Queen to Benares. Meantime the heir-apparent was raised to the throne, and the whole administrative power vested in his minister.

Upon hearing of the installation of his son as Rajah, the old Monarch seemed to evince, for the first and last time in his life, some little interest in proceedings by which he himself was so seriously affected, and the result was a feeble determination not to relinquish his throne without a final struggle. Urged to this course probably by the persuasions of the ambitious and disappointed Ranee, he collected a few followers, and crossed the southern frontier of Nepaul. Jung, however, had received timely notice of his intention, and the luckless King had no sooner encamped in the Nepaul dominions, than he was surprised at night by the troops of the minister, and his small forces utterly routed, four or five hundred remaining killed or wounded upon the field. The Rajah himself was taken prisoner, and placed in confinement by the dutiful son who now occupies the throne, and who sometimes allows him, on grand occasions, to take his seat upon it next to himself.

The vacillating conduct of the imbecile old man throughout his whole reign, the apathy with which he was contented to remain a passive spectator of those bloody dramas of which his court was for so long a period the theatre, deprive him of all claim to commiseration in his present degraded position, which, in fact, is the natural result of his indifference to the game so eagerly played by the contending parties, and of which the stake was his own throne.

If, on the other hand, in a country where common humanity, and still more every kind of principle, is unknown, daring and intrepid conduct merits a reward, Jung has fairly earned for himself the position he now holds; and though his path to greatness has been deluged with the blood of the bravest nobles of the land, it must be admitted that the peace and prosperity which Nepaul now enjoys would never have been possessed by her while distracted and convulsed by the struggles of hostile factions; and much less would she ever have experienced the blessings of an enlightened administration, if these struggles had not resulted in the elevation of General Jung Bahadoor to the office of prime minister.

And now, for the first time in the history of Nepaul, the Durbar was to a certain extent united; internal machinations were no longer to be feared; and the country was ruled over by different members of that family, the elevation of which was due to one of their own number, who possessed sufficient daring and resolution to execute the bold, though unscrupulous schemes his undoubted genius had conceived.

Such was the rapid rise to power at the early age of thirty of General Jung Bahadoor, the Nepaulese ambassador to England, who would have been invested with a deeper interest than the mere colour of his face or brilliancy of his diamonds entitled him to, had the British public known the foregoing particulars of his eventful career. But, perhaps, it was as well for him that they did not, since our occidental notions as to the legitimate method of carrying political measures might have altogether excluded him from the favour of those who delighted to honour him during his visit to England ; but, in extenuation of his conduct, it must be remembered that the mode employed by him of gaining power is the common one in his country, and that his early training had induced a disregard of life and recklessness of consequences ; for he is not, I am convinced, naturally cruel. Impetuous and thoughtless, he has many generous and noble qualities ; and in a companionship of two months I discovered so many estimable traits in him, that I could not help making allowances for the defects in a character entirely self-formed by one ignorant of all moral responsibilities, the half-tamed son of an almost totally uncivilised country.

And while thus unreservedly relating his history, I do so in the belief that he has no desire to conceal what, in his own mind and that of his countrymen, is not regarded as crime, since I have frequently heard him refer, with all the simplicity of conscious innocence, to many of the facts I have related, and for some of which he himself is my authority.

Having thus given a short account of the previous career of this remarkable man, a few words on his present position and future prospects may not be uninteresting, the more so as he purposes, since he has visited the courts of Europe, to become an enlightened ruler of his countrymen.

CHAPTER X.

The titles of his Excellency General Jung Bahadoor Coomaranagee in England—Extraordinary notions of the British public on Indian affairs—Jung Bahadoor's conciliatory policy—Our unsuccessful attempt to penetrate beyond the permitted boundaries—Dangerous position of the Prime Minister—His philanthropic designs—Great opposition on the part of the Durbar—Native punishments—A Nepaulese chief-justice—Jung's popularity with the peasantry and army.

THE rumours in England during Jung Bahadoor's short residence there—of who he was, of what position he held, of his having taken his greatest enemies with him to keep them from conspiring against him while absent—of his being at least a Prince, if not the Rajah himself in disguise—were as far from correct, and as improbable, as were the numerous stories related of him in the newspapers, many of which had no foundation whatever, and in no way redounded to his credit.

The subject, however, of so much speculation was generally too much pleased with his notoriety to care for the means which in some measure obtained it for him ; and I have heard him repeat with great glee some imaginary anecdote of himself, or laughingly enumerate the various appellations by which he had been known. Amongst the few words of English which he could pronounce, were those by which he was most frequently addressed,—such as, the Prince, the Ambassador, your Highness, your Excellency, the Minister, Jung Bahadoor, Jung, or more often "the Jung." Whilst the appearance of the Coomaranagee Polkas showed an unusual amount of correct information on the part of the publisher.

Such ignorance might have been expected from the utter indifference manifested in England towards Indian affairs. The ideas of John Bull upon the subject are often ludicrous in the extreme, as he finds it impossible to divest himself of the preconceived notions which he surely must have been born with when he pertinaciously imagines that all dark-coloured people have woolly heads and thick lips, and speak the broken English of the negro ; nor has he the slightest conception of the relative position of great towns in India, or which States are independent ; or who the Nizam is, or if his contingent is not some part of his dress ; or whether the Taj is not the husband of the Begum mentioned in Pendennis. He has a vague notion that nabobs come from India, and has heard perhaps of cabobs, but what the difference is, or whether they are not articles of Indian export usually packed in casks, he has not the most remote conception. For all the light, therefore, that John Bull could throw upon the subject of who or what Jung Bahadoor was, besides being the Nepaulese ambassador, or where the country was that he came to represent, it might remain a mystery to the present day.

But even supposing the public were better informed on Indian affairs, it would not be a matter of surprise that they should be under a misconception as to what Jung's position in his own country might be, seeing that it is not usual amongst European nations to send their prime ministers on foreign missions. But to estimate correctly the minister's power and authority, the word "send" perhaps ought not to be used in this case, since he was a self-appointed ambassador; and his next brother was left by him to perform the arduous duties attendant on the important office which he vacated for a while.

And now that he is returned to resume the reins of government, and once more become involved in the petty intrigues of his highland court, it is natural that he should look back with delight, not unmingled with regret, at the wonders he has so lately witnessed—the, to him, magical effects of the operations of steam—the still more incomprehensible electric telegraph—our institutions—our court—the magnificence of the successive entertainments, of which he could say "Magna pars fui," and at which he was not more the spectator than the spectacle: but, above all, was it a matter of astonishment to him that such hospitality should have been shown to an unknown and ignorant stranger by a nation whose enterprise is no less stirring than her resources are vast, and in the midst of a social machinery to him so incomprehensibly intricate in its details.

"Why," he would observe after his return to Katmandu, "should I attempt to tell these poor ignorant people what I have seen? It would be as ridiculous in me to suppose they would believe it as it is hopeless to attempt to make them understand it." And he feels that the information he has acquired has been too extensive to allow him to sink to the level of those by whom he is surrounded. But, while anxious to increase his popularity, with his attempts at conciliation is combined a patronizing air, which he cannot conceal, and which is calculated to render him unpopular, even could he bring himself to return to the old system of embracing instead of shaking hands; of taking off his shoes when entering the Durbar; of salaaming ere he addresses his Monarch—all which acts of devotion and homage are repugnant to the man who has had an interview with the Queen of England, and received a visit from the Duke of Wellington. "When that great warrior called upon me," he says, "I felt it to be the proudest moment of my life:" and at Benares, when, upon the occasion of his visiting a native Rajah, there was a question of whether he should go in state or not, he decided the matter by saying, "I shall go just as I went to return the Duke's visit;" or, at another time, "I will receive the Rajah in a friendly way, just as I did the Duke when he called upon me." Nothing seemed to impress him so deeply as the absence of all display where genuine greatness rendered it unnecessary; and he looks with no slight contempt upon the pomp to which he in common with his court was formerly so much attached. That court, however, retaining of course its old unenlightened sentiments, looks with suspicion and distrust on the independent manners of the returned prime minister. "He has become a Feringhee."—"He wants to introduce their barbarous customs amongst us."—"He brings visitors, and is making friends with the English, in order to betray us to them." This is said by his enemies at court; and, while they watch his every action, esteem him a traitor, who, if they did but know it, is the best friend of their country. Thus, in spite of his earnest desire to promote its welfare, he is likely to be thwarted, and his ardent and somewhat impatient temperament will not, it is to be feared, improve matters, however good his intentions may be. That he is already careful lest he offend any prejudices, I had a convincing and most annoying proof.

On the journey through India, while in high spirits, out shooting, he had promised to allow us to travel over any part of Nepaul we might wish to visit—a permission never yet granted to any European. To the fulfilment of this promise we naturally looked with no small pleasure ; but, after a residence of a week in Nepaul, the anti-Anglican feeling was so strongly manifested, that the mere fact of four or five European visitors having been in Katmandu (for Lord G—— and his party were among his guests) brought upon him a certain degree of odium.

To allow strangers to visit Nepaul, and reside at Katmandu, was unusual, but bearable ; the idea of a common beef-eater infringing the limits of a circle beyond which no British resident, much less traveller, had ever penetrated, was so monstrous a heresy on the part of the prime minister—so serious an infraction of a well-established rule—that even Jung felt it to be too unpopular an act by which to celebrate his return to his country. It was with much regret that we were obliged to relinquish so interesting an enterprise. I must not, however, forget his offer to adhere to his promise if we wished it, saying at the same time that his doing so would seriously compromise him. But, as *compromise* and *decapitate* may be looked upon as synonymous terms in Nepaul, we felt that it was hardly fair to our kind host to place him in such an awkward position ; and as, moreover, the effect of his being so compromised in Katmandu would have probably entailed upon us a precisely similar fate, we considered it hardly fair to the guests either. But while thus hanging back from his promise on the score of compromising himself, I am fully persuaded that personal considerations had but little to do in the matter. He is looking out for means of usefulness, and it was more the fear of retarding his schemes of improvement by thus increasing the popular discontent that induced him to change his mind, than any hope of retaining his head upon his shoulders. The difficulty of doing this can be but very slightly increased; and it must be admitted that he esteems life as lightly in his own case as he formerly did when others were concerned.

It cannot but be regretted that with so pure an object he should be totally without co-operation from any quarter. The young King, capable only of aiding in nefarious schemes, such as those already recounted, can in no way comprehend the new-fangled philanthropic views of the prime minister. He cares little about the welfare of his country; his amusement seems to consist in concocting and executing bloody designs, and his mind must be so accustomed to this species of excitement that it can scarce do without it. It is unfortunate that the Rajah's hobby should lie in this peculiar direction, more unfortunate still that the contemplated victim should be Jung; for I presume that there is little doubt that the King's brother, who was engaged in the last conspiracy against the minister's life—which took place a few days after my visit—must have acted with the knowledge, and most probably at the instigation, of his Majesty.

Nor can Jung look to his brothers for support as in times of old: one of them, whom he esteemed amongst the most faithful, was, as before mentioned, deeply implicated in the same attempt on his life; and there is no one now on whom he can confidently depend in the hour of need except the two youngest of the family, who accompanied him to England, and whom I consider thoroughly devoted to his interests. Deserted by his King, who owes his throne to him, his life conspired against by one of his own brothers, bound to him by the yet stronger ties of blood, he stands alone a mark for the dagger of any one who would win the approval of his degraded Sovereign. But his bearing is not the less bold, or his eye less piercing, as he makes the man quail before him who is that moment planning his destruction. He anticipates the fate of his fourteen predecessors; they were all assassinated! His predecessors, however, did not surround themselves with a guard armed with rifles always loaded.* In all probability the man who takes the life of the prime minister will do so at the price of his own. So securely

* The arms of his body-guard were bought in London, of Purdy, Lancaster, and other eminent rifle makers, and cost Jung about 2000*l.*

guarded is he, and so careful of his own safety, that I cannot but hope he may live to frustrate the designs of his enemies, and to carry out that enlightened policy which, while it morally elevates the people, would develop the resources of a country possessing many natural advantages, in its delightful climate, fertile soil, and industrious population. Valleys unvisited by civilization save as received through the medium of a few semi-barbarous travellers, may contain treasures which they are now unknown to possess; mines of copper, lead, and antimony, now clumsily worked, may be made to yield of their abundance; tracts of uncultivated lands be brought into rich cultivation, and efficient means of transport would carry their produce far and wide through the country. Katmandu itself would be on the high road for the costly trade of Chinese Tartary and Thibet with the provinces of Upper India.

In fact it is impossible to enumerate the various benefits which would accrue to the country were a different system of government adopted; and it is much to be feared that unless the present prime minister lives to accomplish the task he has undertaken, no one of his successors, for some time to come at least, will have either the will or the ability requisite for its successful consummation.

In some of his legislative acts Jung had shown himself to be in advance of his age before he left Nepaul. No less than twenty-two punishments for various crimes, principally consisting of different modes of torture, were abolished. A thief must have been three times convicted of the crime ere he can suffer the penalty entailed upon the offence, viz., loss of his hand ; and after it is cut off, he has his choice between having it bound up or allowing himself to bleed to death. I understood the latter alternative to be the one usually chosen by the culprit. Gambling is strictly prohibited in Nepaul, except for four or five days during the celebration of the Devali.

Women are not liable to capital punishment. The mutilation of noses no longer exists, although some years ago it was the most usual punishment, and one village was entirely peopled by the unfortunate victims of such barbarous treatment.

The amount of labour which his position as prime minister entails upon Jung is almost incredible ; the simplest bargain cannot be struck, nor a cooly engaged, nor can a departure or an arrival take place, without his sign manual. In fact he comprises within himself the whole of the ministry, besides doing the entire duty of the several departments, and the office of premier in Nepaul can be no more a sinecure than it is in England. One can only wonder that a position fraught with such imminent danger to its possessor, and bringing upon him such incessant trouble and responsibility, should be so eagerly sought, when it entails the almost absolute certainty of a violent death. With us moral courage is an indispensable quality for a prime minister; in Nepaul, physical courage is no less needed. If he is a good shot, and expert with his kukri and kora, so much the better for him. As regards both these accomplishments Jung was eminently qualified for the post he now holds; but his literary acquirements were of a very low order, for upon becoming prime minister he could neither read nor write. Finding great inconvenience from his incapacity in these respects, he applied himself diligently to his alphabet, and was soon able to carry on all official correspondence of any importance to himself. The whole of the political, fiscal, and judicial communications are submitted to him, and the departments controlled by him, very little regard being had to the Rajah's will on the subject.

The next officer in rank to Jung Bahadoor is his brother, Bum Bahadoor, who bears the mark on his hand of the horrible action in Durbar already recorded. He appeared inferior in ability to his brother, but it is difficult to judge of the talent of any one who is in a subordinate position in Nepaul.

The Raj Guru is the highest spiritual dignitary in Nepaul, and in that capacity received the greatest deference from every one, including Jung, whose popularity in some measure rests on his intimate relations with the chief priest, to whom he invariably paid every mark of respect. The Raj Guru met us at Benares, and granted indulgences to those who had visited England. So great is the respect shown him, that upon entering his presence the prime minister invariably touched with his forehead the foot of the holy man. To the office of spiritual adviser to the Rajah is added that of judge of the spiritual court, which is one of great emolument, arising chiefly from fines levied on the infraction of religious ceremonies or ordinances—such as the killing or maltreating of a cow and other like enormities.

Next in order follow the Kazies, or "Patres conscripti," who ought to possess some voice in the administration of affairs, but are content to remain silent during the independent rule of the Minister Sahib. They number thirty or forty, and their duty is to consult upon all weighty matters connected with the Government, while some act as governors of provinces, others as judges in important causes.

Then come the Sirdars, who also decide causes, and possess considerable authority in the more remote districts, governing some of the provinces, and superintending the collection of revenue. Their number is far larger than that of the Kazies.

We visited the supreme court one day and saw the Chief-justice, or Durma Dikar, sitting cross-legged (smoking his hookah on the verandah), the court having adjourned. The old man bore that venerable appearance which is everywhere esteemed inseparable from the judicial character, and I doubted whether his long grey beard was not a more imposing, as it certainly was a more natural and graceful appendage than a wig.

There are six law courts in Katmandu, presided over by Sirdars and Bicharees, and the laws and modes of punishment are very effectual for the prevention of crime; for although a prisoner cannot be convicted except upon his own confession, he may be subjected to an ordeal which will most probably extort it; and, perhaps, in an eastern country justice is more effectually administered by such methods than where the judge decides on the guilt or innocence of a man by speculating on the character of the witnesses, and believing those who look most as if they were telling the truth; and where, although he knows that all the witnesses are more or less bribed, he is not allowed to take any but a voluntary admission from the prisoner, when perhaps a little gentle persuasion would save a great deal of unnecessary trouble, to say nothing of the amount of lying that might thus be dispensed with. Whatever the laws may be, they seem to give perfect satisfaction to the inhabitants, who cannot be called a litigious race.

While we were at Bisoleah, on our way to Katmandu, an interesting instance occurred of the prime minister taking the law into his own hands; and, as far as we could judge, complete justice was done to the parties. A complaint was preferred by a deputation of the peasantry of the Terai against one of the sirdars who was a member of his suite, and who had been governor of some part of the district before he had accompanied the minister on his expedition to England. It was alleged that he had, in connexion with his brother, who was an especial favourite with Jung, defrauded them of 25,000 rupees. This charge was indignantly denied by the two sirdars. The case was fully entered into, and the result was, that Jung became convinced of the justice of the claim of the peasantry. He had no sooner satisfied himself on this point than he ordered both the noblemen to be placed in confinement, where they were to remain until the required sum was forthcoming. The affair delayed us twenty-four hours; and I perfectly well remember wondering at the time what could be the cause of a detention for so long a period in so unpleasant a locality; more especially as by it we lost the chance of a day's rhinoceros shooting, which was, doubtless, as great a disappointment to Jung as to myself.

By thus carefully protecting the interests of the peasantry he has endeared himself to them, since they are always sure of a ready and attentive hearing of any complaint, although it may affect the highest nobles in the land. In talking to a man who acted as guide on our return through the Terai, we discovered that the popularity of Jung, arising from this cause, had extended across the frontier, and had induced my informant to migrate into the Nepaul dominions, so that he might benefit by the paternal rule of its prime minister. He said the taxes were lighter, and he led altogether a more happy and independent life than in the Company's dominions, where the native officers employed as tax-gatherers do not always display the most scrupulous honesty.

But it is not with the peasantry alone that Jung is so deservedly a favourite. With the soldiers he is, if possible, still more popular. An admirer of Napoleon, he has profited by the perusal of his life, and turns to advantage his knowledge of the influence possessed in so wonderful a manner by one whom he seeks in every respect to imitate, so far as the difference of position admits. That he has succeeded admirably with the army there is no doubt. His personal feats of daring and known courage are considerable aids to an imitation of the more scientific means employed by his great model.

Thus, firmly seated in the affections of the most important portions of the community over which he rules with unlimited power, and a most ardent wish to improve their condition, it will be on all accounts most deplorable if the country is deprived of the services of so valuable a man by some vile plot, emanating from the petty intrigue of a jealous and disappointed Durbar.

CHAPTER XI.

The temple of Balajee—The old Newar capital—The houses and temples of Patn—View from the city gates—Nepaulese festivals—The Newars skilful artisans—The arsenal—The magazine and cannon-foundry.

ONE afternoon we strolled across some verdant meadows, and along narrow shady avenues, to visit the temple of Balajee. There is nothing in the building itself worthy of notice; but near it is a tank of beautifully clear water, filled with sacred fishes, which crowd near the visitor as he stands on the brink, expecting to be fed with grain, which some old women at the gate sell for their especial benefit. Balajee is one of those sheltered nooks which make the scenery of Nepaul so attractive. Immediately under a wooded knoll the trees dip into a tank, from whence the water leaps in three tiny cascades into the courtyard of the temple, quaint and singular itself, and rendered still more interesting from its connexion with the sacred fonts and groves near which it is so romantically situated.

Hitherto we had seen no Newar town. Katmandu, the capital of Nepaul, was built by the conquering Ghorkas, and is comparatively modern. The old Newar capital is Patn: situated on a green slope, and fortified by a high wall, it looks picturesque when seen from the modern city, from which it is distant about two miles.

Crossing the narrow brick bridge which spans the Bhagmutty, outside the walls of the town, we shortly after entered the massive old gates of the ancient capital. As we trotted past the high rickety houses, along the brick pavement of the narrow streets, still slippery from the morning dew, we encountered troops of girls with garlands in their hair, for this was some festive day. At the corners of the streets were beings of both sexes, as decrepit as the houses under which they crouched, presiding over baskets full of beautiful flowers. The entire population were Newars, except a few fierce, mustachioed Ghorkas, who stood sentinels over the temples, or loitered about the guardhouse. The long street looked deserted ; there was not a single shop in it ; and the foot-passengers were few and far between. But the grand square was the chief feature of the place, and was well worthy of a visit. We looked with astonishment and delight at the incongruous mass of buildings, of the most varied and fantastic construction, yet massive and substantial ; but whence the designs originated, or in what other part of the known world anything is to be seen approaching to the style of Newar architecture, it would be impossible to conjecture. Houses built of horn are said to exist at Lassa ; and from Lassa, I should imagine, came the designs for the temples and houses of Patn. Time has mellowed their bright colours—if they were ever painted at all like those at Katmandu—into a sombre, quiet grey. The Durbar, a huge, massive building, is absolutely covered with black wood-carving. The care displayed in its execution is still apparent through the mass of dust and cobwebs which almost conceal it; for the old Durbar of Patn is deserted. The residence of the monarchs who ruled the happy valley is in strong contrast with the smiling appearance of their former territory. It alone seems to have gone into mourning for its former occupants, while the valley seems to thrive as well under the rule of the Ghorkas as it did under that of the Newars. The Durbar is of great extent, and occupies one side of the square, in the centre of which stand two monoliths, between 30 and 40 feet high: on one of them is the figure of an angel, represented in all respects as angels usually are, with the addition of a magnificent gilt tail; this, together with a pair of large gilt wings, gave it a most gorgeous appearance. My Ghorka guide could give me no information as to what particular divinity this figure was intended to represent. The other pillar was crowned by the figure of a Newar monarch with an unpronounceable name, who was watched over by a cobra, standing upon its tail, and looking over his head with its mouth wide open.

On the opposite side to that on which the Durbar was situated were two temples: one of them, built of grey sandstone, was an imposing structure, altogether different from any building, lay or ecclesiastical, that I had ever seen before. The lower story consisted of massive verandahs or cloisters; the pillars were all of grey sandstone, very simple in form; and the connecting arch was somewhat Saracenic in its appearance. The temple was square, and the corridor which ran round it was elevated considerably above the level of the court: the ascent to it was by two flights of steps, each guarded by a pair of sculptured winged lions. Three stories of light belfry-like temples, three upon each side of the square, surmounted each other in rows; in the centre was a mass of architecture between a dome and a spire, rising to a height of upwards of 100 feet above the level of the court: the whole formed a pyramidal structure ornamented with fantastic devices, and undoubtedly Bhuddist in its character.

The other temple was a two-storied pagoda; its bright colours were faded, and it appeared far inferior to those of more recent construction. There were also ruined pyramidal shrines of no known architecture, and difficult to describe from their complicated nature—antique specimens of the masonry of ages long gone by, and memorials of a religion doubtless impure, although Bhuddist in its character and origin.

No less singular were the residences of the old Newar nobility, a race which no longer exists, and the only remains of which now extant are their ruined habitations, evidently destined to succumb before long to the same all-destroying power which has long since obliterated every trace of their former owners.

How different was the peculiar yet handsome style which distinguished the dwellings of the Newar nobles at Patn from the tawdry glitter which characterises the mansions of the present Ghorka chiefs in the modern capital! Here the carving is more rich, the ornaments more massive, the houses themselves are more lofty and capacious. Sometimes two or three elaborately-carved balconies adorn the sombre but not less imposing exterior; from the projecting eaves wooden tassels, forming a sort of fringe, swing to and fro over the windows.

The roofs are beautifully tiled, each tile having a double curvature, while the corners of the buildings are quaintly turned up, giving a Chinese look to the building. The whole appearance of the houses and temples carries one far from the mud-huts or close cities of the plains of India, into the land of chopsticks and small feet, and the traveller feels much nearer to Pekin than to Calcutta as he wanders along the empty streets under the frowning houses and indescribable temples of the Newar town of Patn.

Everything seemed to have been blighted by time; besides all the old temples, old houses, old gates, and old streets, there were numbers of old people. Everything seemed to sympathise with everything else, and had evidently come to the conclusion that there was nothing worth living for, and the sooner they all took themselves off and quitted the bright valley of Nepaul the better. And indeed it was difficult to realize the existence of anything half so cheerful inside the town as the prospect which met our view as we emerged from its gloomy entrance, and looked upon the luxuriant plain, the glittering capital shining in its midst, whose gaudy pagodas, hung round with bells and adorned with flags, were very different from those just visited; the industrious population were going light-hearted to their work as we rode through smiling fields, and we ceased to wonder at Patn looking deserted, for it was evident that all the cheerfully disposed inhabitants had flitted away, unable to bear its depressing influence, and leaving behind them only the crabbed old people at the corners of the streets, and the tattered beggars, who must make a meagre livelihood out of the falling temples and 24,000 rotten houses of the once handsome capital of Nepaul.

It was a clear frosty morning, and, as we rode down the gentle slope on which the old city stands, the snowy range of the Himalaya burst upon us with inexpressible grandeur. The Gosain-than, a mass of glistening snow, looked contemptuously down upon the Jibjibia, itself covered with snow: though 13,000 feet lower than the Gosain-than, the Jibjibia in turn overtopped the Sheopoorie, which rises abruptly from the valley to a height of 2000 feet. On a peninsula, formed by the junction of the Bhagmutty and Bishmutty, stands the town of Katmandu, surrounded by a high wall in which are four gates: to the east the snow-capped peaks extend as far as the eye can reach; to the west the Dawalogiri, the highest mountain in the world, is in clear weather distinctly visible; in that direction the valley is shut in by lofty hills, the steepest of which is crossed by the Chandanagiri pass.

The exhilarating effect of so glorious a scene seemed not to be lost upon the inhabitants themselves, and we observed among them the same merry and contented appearance as that which is so remarkable amongst the inhabitants of Switzerland and the Tyrol; indeed mountaineers in general either have much fewer troubles than lowlanders, or take them less to heart.

The Nepaulese, in common with most highland tribes, have strong religious feelings, and are bigoted adherents to a faith which they would find it somewhat difficult to define. One use to which they put their religion, and in which they far exceed even the Roman Catholics of the Alps, is, in making it furnish them with an almost unlimited number of holidays and festivals: no opportunity of merry-making is lost by the light-hearted inhabitants of Nepaul, and in this respect they are at once distinguishable from their more gloomy and saturnine conquerors, the Ghorkas, who, glorying only in the art of war, look with contempt on what they consider the frivolity of the Newars.

There can be no doubt of the warlike character of the Ghorkas, even had not our own experience testified to the fact in a most unpleasant way. Not only are they brave and skilful soldiers, but, for a barbarous nation, they are wonderfully advanced in the art of fabricating the implements of war; they cast their own ordnance, manufacture their own muskets, shot, powder, and cartridge-boxes; in fact, every instrument or weapon used in civilized warfare is manufactured in Nepaul, often clumsily enough, but the mere fact of their being capable of being used, and used with effect, is highly creditable to the ingenuity of the Ghorkas.

The Newars are still more skilful artisans than the Ghorkas, but their talent does not lie in the same direction. The bricks of Nepaul are deservedly famed; whether the virtue lies in the clay of which they are formed, or the skill with which they are made, I do not know—most probably in both. The Newars excel also in bell-making; it is the trade of the land; they are all bellmakers from their youth, and proofs of their skill are exhibited hanging at the corners of pagodas, swinging from the roofs of houses, surmounting Dagobas—in fact, the device upon a

Nepaulese banner should be a bell. In jewellery they are no less expert, and are elaborate workmen in all metals. A species of coarse paper is manufactured by them from the bark of a tree, which is first reduced to a pulp and then spread over a sheet and dried.

They are as excellent agriculturists as tradesmen, and the rich soil of the valley is not allowed by the industrious peasants to lie fallow a moment longer than is necessary.

At certain seasons every inhabitant capable of wielding the hoe is at work, and there is much incentive to such industry, for the soil is inexhaustible, and seems as if it could go on for an indefinite period yielding its four crops a year—namely, wheat, rice, Indian corn, and vegetables—supporting thereby a double population. The plough is never used. It struck me that the introduction of buffaloes from the plains would be advantageous in assisting the worthy Newar, whose religious scruples prevent his using the bullock. There is a species of small buffalo, which is a native of the Himalayas, but it is never brought down by the Bhootyas into the plains, nor even to Katmandu.

We went one day to visit the arsenal, which a veteran of the Nepaul army took an especial delight in exhibiting, and naturally looked for expressions of wonder and delight from the barbarians. But the only astonishment we felt was, that such a mass of fire-arms, so excessively old and so excessively dirty, should be thought worthy of being carefully ranged throughout the long dark rooms. In a corner of one of these rooms the light streamed brightly through a window on some old-fashioned firelocks bearing an English maker's name; they were trophies of the war with the British, and were held worthy of conspicuous places in the Nepaul arsenal. The delighted old Colonel pointed these out to us with a laudable pride; he said the arsenal contained 100,000 stand of arms, and expected us to believe it. Had they been in proper order, the collection would have been of importance numerically considered.

Their artillery was insignificant, but they possessed trophies denied to many more powerful nations in a pair of brass 2-pounders, also taken from the British in the same disastrous campaign. I looked as abashed and mortified as I could, and pleased the Colonel exceedingly thereby. In the same establishment was carried on the process of manufacturing powder of a very coarse grain, and we were shown sundry store-rooms containing grape and canister.

Leaving the arsenal, we mounted our elephants, crossed the parade-ground and the river, and, passing through the massive gateway, reached the magazine, situated in the interior of the city, where we had an opportunity of witnessing the process of hammering iron into balls. The Nepaulese can produce no heat sufficient to cast balls, and are, consequently, obliged to beat them into the required shape, an almost endless operation. By this tedious process the making of each two-pound ball occupies two men a whole day, and costs, including other incidental charges, about a rupee, so that the expenses of a siege would come rather heavy upon the Government. All round the courtyard blacksmiths were forging and hammering, while in the middle of it a number of men were employed beating leather, so as to render it sufficiently pliable to undergo the process of being trodden soft, a curious operation, and fatiguing to the muscles of any other legs than those of the Nepaulese, who keep continually doubling up the leather and treading it out again, and putting their feet to all sorts of uses, in which, if we had properly cultivated the gifts of nature, we should, doubtless, be equally skilled. At present our great object is to make our feet look smaller than they naturally are, and even in that the Chinese excel us, civilized though we be. The result of so much beating and treading, was a number of leather cartridge-boxes, which could not have been harder had they been deal; so the means did not justify the end, and perhaps after all we make better use of our feet than the Nepaulese tanners do.

In another part of the establishment was a gang of men engaged in twisting gun-barrels, turning out wonderful productions, considering the rude method employed.

The stocks were more easily fabricated, and the whole musket justified the pride with which it was exhibited; but Jung is no longer satisfied with the productions of the Nepaulese gunmakers. He visited a gun-manufactory at Birmingham, and was most disagreeably surprised by finding how different was the English mode of manufacturing the implements of war from that employed in Nepaul.

In England Jung had seen brass guns cast by the score during his short visit to the foundry. Here they were being cast at the rate of one every two or three months. The metal is not allowed to run into the mould in a continuous stream, but is ladled in, thereby rendering the gun liable to flaws. There were many other improvements which it would have been obvious to a practised eye were needed in the gun-factory of Nepaul; and it was plain enough that everything was rough and clumsy; but Jung had paid especial attention to these subjects while in England, and intends speedily to introduce an improved system. How long it will be ere he will have a steam-foundry established in Katmandu time alone can show.

CHAPTER XII.

Kindness of the Mahila Sahib—His motive—Drawing-room ornaments—Visit to the palace of Jung Bahadoor—A trophy of the London season—Grand Durbar at the reading of the Queen of England's letter—Dress of the officers—Review of troops—Dancing boys.

THE Mahila Sahib, the younger brother of his Majesty, was a very pleasant-looking young man, with a much more amiable expression of countenance than his royal brother, and professed to be one of Jung's greatest friends and allies. As a compliment to the minister, he politely requested us to pay him a visit, an invitation of which we were glad to avail ourselves, since it proved his kindly feeling towards our host, whilst it gave us an opportunity of inspecting the ménage of a Nepaulese Prince Royal.

It is worth while to make a trip to Nepaul, not only for the delight of viewing the romantic beauty of its scenery, of wondering at the stupendous height of its mountains, of roaming amidst its ancient cities, ruined palaces, and glittering pagodas, but in order to take a lesson in human nature, for we are not at liberty to suppose that the princes and nobles of this country are a more depraved class than any other body of men, the fact being that a Nepaulese follows his natural impulses, unfettered by the restraints of our standard of civilization and morality, and the results are apparent. Is not the more civilized inhabitant of western lands actuated by the same feelings, and would he not behave in the same manner as his swarthy brother in the East, had he been brought up in the same code of morality, and were he as fearless of the consequences of his following the bent of his own inclination? But if so, then the visitor to Nepaul simply sees the game of human life played openly and unconstrainedly, and in no way hampered by the rules which prevail in more civilized countries; and the unsophisticated tyro has only to come here and learn in a month what would cost him a lifetime of anxious study in a country enjoying the blessings of civilization.

The palace of the Mahila Sahib is situated in a court-yard, and is entered by a small doorway, by no means in keeping with the handsome staircase, lined with muskets, up which we followed the prince, who had come to the entrance to meet us. We were ushered into a long narrow room, similar in shape to the reception-room in all other Nepaulese palaces, and adorned in like manner with a profusion of pictures, occidental as well as oriental, while in the midst, upon a round table, and displayed as drawing-room ornaments, was an incongruous collection of articles, amongst which I remarked three leaden spoons, an old cruet-stand, a Bohemian glass scent-bottle, an old hair-brush and tooth-brush on some hot-water plates, a pair of brass candlesticks, and other wares usually found in kitchens, pantries, and bedrooms. Some English prints and pictures of a particularly pothouse appearance attracted me into a little side room, where a handsome telescope stood pointed out of the open window, from which there was a lovely and extensive view, and while my friend and the prince were chatting in the next room I took advantage of the means thus afforded me of enjoying the prospect.

On looking through the telescope the first object which met my eye was the roof of a handsome house, on which figures were moving briskly to and fro. All the windows of this mansion were commanded by the glass, and I almost imagined I could see the female figures flitting about in the more gloomy and secluded part, which seemed to be the harem. The house thus under observation struck me as being known to me, and upon looking at the neighbouring objects I perceived that it was the palace of the Minister Sahib.

The fact of the glass being thus pointed to his house was in itself a suspicious circumstance, but I little thought that the bland owner of the leaden spoons and pothouse pictures was then deliberately contemplating the vile plot he so soon afterwards nearly succeeded in executing.

Within a week after this visit I heard that our polite entertainer was in confinement for an attempt to assassinate the minister, towards whom he had so recently professed the profoundest sentiments of regard.

We descended into the well laid-out garden attached to the palace and devoured the delicious mandarin oranges, with which hundreds of trees were loaded, until our attention was diverted from them by a luscious fruit, in appearance something like a medlar : this fruit is rare in Nepaul, the tree being a native of Thibet.

It cost us an effort to bid adieu to the polite prince and his attractive garden ; but at length we remounted our elephants and proceeded on our way to the Minister's house. Passing through the handsome gateway, guarded by a magnificent tiger, that prowled restlessly up and down his cage, a vigilant-looking sentinel, we entered a yard filled with the soldiers and retainers of the illustrious man whom we had come to visit.

We were greeted cordially by the Minister Sahib, who was surrounded by a crowd of brothers, only three of whom I knew, viz. the two fat travellers and the future would-be assassin.

Jung's house was a large white building, which looked as if a Chinaman had mixed together a Birmingham factory and an Italian villa, every now and then throwing in a strong dash of the style of his own country by way of improvement. It is three stories high, and one wing is devoted to the six "beautiful missises" who compose the female part of his establishment.

The state-room was very similar in shape and appearance to that in the palace of the Mahila Sahib, but was, if possible, still more fantastically ornamented. A picture of her Majesty's Coronation was supported on the one side by a lady's bonnet, on the other by a carpet-bag, while a lady's riding-habit, an officer's red jacket, and various other articles of attire were hung round the walls upon pegs ; here and there, perhaps partly hidden by the folds of a lady's dress, was to be seen the portrait of some sedate old Nepaulese noble.

Jung called our attention to one of these ; it was the portrait of a strikingly handsome man, whose keen eye and lofty brow seemed almost to entitle him to the position he held between the Duke of Wellington and the Queen. "See," said Jung, enthusiastically, "here is the Queen of England, and she has not got a more loyal subject than I am." Then turning to the picture of the man with the keen eyes and high forehead, he remarked, "That is my poor uncle Mahtibar Singh, whom I shot; it is very like him." After which he launched into a discussion upon the comparative merits of the Duke of Wellington and Napoleon, and, skipping two cocked hats and a bonnet, went on to some Purdy's rifles, of which he spoke in glowing terms and with all the enthusiasm of a true sportsman.

My friend Colonel Dhere Shum Shere now came up, whistling the Sturm Marsch, and challenged me to a game of billiards: he was in his manner more thoroughly English than any native I ever knew, and both in appearance and disposition looked as if he was an Anglo-Saxon who had been dyed by mistake. When in Europe he used to dress like an Englishman, and in company with his brother, the Minister Sahib, in similar attire, patronized Vauxhall, Cremorne, and other places of fashionable resort usually frequented by such fast men as they showed themselves to be. Like Jung, he used to say he could not bear the abominable screeching at the Opera, and consequently never made his appearance until the commencement of the ballet, which was much more in their line.

Having profited by his visits to European houses, Jung intends to show his enlightenment by substituting pictures for the articles of vertu with which the walls of his room are at present adorned, and to exchange kitchen ware for albums, in order to prove that he has travelled to some purpose. While examining these table ornaments, I observed a civilized looking little square piece of satin, and on taking it up found

I was inspecting the first invitation to Her Majesty's Opera that had ever reached Nepaul.

In one apartment 700*l.* worth of ladies' dresses, purchased in England, were spread upon the floor, destined, I presume, to adorn some sable beauties on whom the fashionable flounces of Madame Devy would be anything but becoming.

Jung informed us that a grand ceremony was to take place on the following day. The Queen of England's letter, of which he was the bearer, was to be read in full Durbar under a salute of twenty-one guns—a greater honour than is shown even to a communication from his Imperial Majesty of the celestial empire.

We accordingly repaired at the appointed hour next morning to the palace of the King, in the great square of Katmandu, and were ushered into the narrow room appropriated to the Durbar. It was hung round with pictures that a tavern would be ashamed of, and altogether looked so dirty that, had it been a tavern, it would have had but little custom.

Seated on a throne were the two Kings gorgeously apparelled and bedizened with jewels, while the Minister Sahib wore nothing but the simple bukkoo, or fur-robe, of great value but unassuming appearance.

There was to be a review of the troops after Durbar, and, as nearly all the nobility of Nepaul hold rank in the army, the whole assemblage was in uniform, certainly one of the most dazzling that I ever saw collected together. Each man had twice as many feathers as he was entitled to wear, and, while their cocked hats were always completely hid, the bodies of the more diminutive officers almost shared the same fate. The English dragoon and the French hussar might here recognize portions of their uniform, adorned with gold and silver lace to an extent which field-marshals alone have, with us, a right to indulge in, and often mixed up with some Oriental finery—a pair of glittering slippers that consorted but ill with the tightly strapped-down gold lace trowsers, or a handsome shawl that clumsily supported the jewelled sabre.

The ceremony of presentation having been gone through, a select party, consisting of the two Kings, the English Resident and one or two officers of the Embassy, and the Prime Minister, adjourned to an upper room. This seemed to me a curious proceeding, and one which the remaining portion of the legislators must have thought particularly unsatisfactory: however they looked as if they did not care, or could not help it; and while the coterie above were solemnly perusing Her Majesty's epistle, and the guns were booming in honour of it, we below were chatting upon indifferent matters, until the

Royal party returned, when, in addition to the pawn usually given on such occasions, we were presented by their Majesties with some Nepaulese weapons, and amidst more firing of cannon left the palace in the Minister's phaëton to witness a grand review.

The parade-ground was situated immediately under the city walls, and upon it 6000 men were drawn up: the uniforms differed in some instances; the "rifles" were in a pea-green suit which hung about them loosely, while the regiments of the line wore red coats, with trowsers ample enough to please a Turk. Upon their turbans or caps were the distinguishing badges of their respective corps—a half-moon, a lion, the sun, and various other devices. The regiments were not numbered as with us, but adopted some magniloquent high-sounding title suggestive of their valour in war, fearlessness of danger, and other martial qualities.

There was no cavalry, the country not being adapted to that arm of the service, but the artillery seemed very fairly handled; there was an immense deal of firing, both of small arms and great guns, which I believe was very good; and there were a great number of evolutions performed, which, as I am not a soldier, did not seem to me more incomprehensible than such manœuvring usually is, but I was informed by those who were capable of judging, that in this instance they really were altogether without meaning. Regiment after regiment marched past, the men swinging their arms regularly as they moved, and trying to persuade themselves they were British grenadiers. At all events the band was playing that tune. Suddenly the music changed ; they struck up a lively polka, and a number of little boys in a sort of penwiper costume, clasping one another like civilized ladies and gentlemen, began to caper about, after which they went through various antics that surpassed even the wildest notions of our highly civilized community : all this while the troops were manœuvring as vehemently as ever, and the boys were dancing as fantastically ; and the whole thing was so eminently ridiculous and looked so very like a farce, that it was difficult to maintain that dignified and sedate appearance which was expected from the spectators of a scene so imposing.

Jung alone looked for no expressions of surprise or admiration from us, but was evidently disappointed and chagrined at the inferiority of his own soldiers to those he had seen in Europe and amongst our Indian troops. He could indeed point with pride to the stalwart bearing and soldierlike appearance of his men, but he had seen "the Guards" reviewed, he had been present at an inspection of 15,000 of the French army at Versailles, and he seemed half ashamed of the display we were witnessing, notwithstanding our efforts to comfort him by telling him that we had little thought the art of war was so far advanced in the wild valleys and rocky mountains of Nepaul.

CHAPTER XIII.

Distinguishing features of the races of Nepaul—The Ghorkas—Conquest by them of Katmandu—Maintenance of the Nepaul army—Beem Singh's monument—A feast at the minister's—We bid him adieu—Ascent of the Sheopoori—Magnificent view of the Himalayas from its summit.

THE grand review over, we availed ourselves of the opportunity to inspect the regiments composed of men recruited in some of the most distant provinces of Nepaul. They bore in their countenances little resemblance either to the Ghorkas or Newars. We examined their faces, and tried to imagine what sort of a looking country was likely to produce this sort of a looking man. A regiment of dark-visaged stalwart Ghorkas would march past, followed by a diminutive race from the north-western frontier, little, ill-made, and abominably ugly. The same cast of countenance was prevalent throughout the regiments that had been recruited there ; all the men had the same high cheek-bones, or wide mouths, or whatever their peculiarity might be. The insignificant Newars looked majestic by the side of these men, while in their turn their own strong Chinese characteristics were thrown completely into the shade by some regiment from the north-east, almost pure Bootyan or Mongolian.

There are not, however, many Newars employed as soldiers, and the army is chiefly composed of Muggurs, Gurungs, and Krats. These tribes differ only in their religion, according as it combines in a greater or less degree the superstitions of the Hindoo worship with those of Bhuddism. But none of these races differed from one another more completely than did the Ghorka from them all; he was the only man among them born to be a soldier, and he looked with contempt upon the mongrel races that surrounded him.

The country from which he himself originally sprang is nevertheless a matter of speculation; he certainly is not of trans-Himalayan origin, but no doubt the comfortable life he leads in Nepaul prevents his caring to inquire whence he came. The Rajah claims descent from the Rajput princes. The capital town of the country from which they descended into the valley of Nepaul is Ghorka, situated about fifty miles westward of Katmandu. The Ghorkas had already possessed themselves of the whole territory to the westward for some hundred of miles until their border touched the kingdom of Runjeit Singh and the vale of Cashmere; they then turned their conquering arms eastward in 1716; and, overrunning the valleys of the Newars, their progress was only arrested on the Sikkim frontier.

The conquest of the valley of Katmandu was

attended with circumstances of the greatest barbarity; thousands of the inhabitants were starved to death by the Ghorka King, Prithi Naraim. There were then in Nepaul a few Christians, converted by a Jesuit mission. These were all compelled to fly the country, some taking refuge in Thibet, others crossing our frontier and settling at Bettiah, where a Christian community at present exists. Not long after he had conquered Nepaul, the Ghorka monarch organized an expedition into Tartary, which was so signally successful that the H'Lassa Government was obliged to treat on humiliating conditions. This advantage was followed, in defiance of the treaty, by another invasion, which was only arrested by the forces of the Emperor, who, having heard of the violent proceedings in this distant part of his dominions, sent an army of 70,000 men to oppose the Ghorka invaders, who were completely overwhelmed, and obliged to retreat. The Chinese followed the retiring force across their own frontier, and not until they had reached the valley of Noyakot, eighteen miles from Katmandu, did they consent to treat for peace, which was now humbly sued for by the Ghorka king.

Not satisfied with serving as soldiers in their own country, the Ghorkas have offered their services to the Indian Government, and two of its finest regiments are composed of soldiers of this race.

No European, as far as I could learn, has ever yet penetrated to their city, which however can contain no object of very great attraction, since it must want those Chinese peculiarities which render Katmandu and Patn so interesting, and must more nearly resemble the large cities of the plains. It has a large population, is well built and fortified, and is situated on a commanding eminence.

The Nepaul army is maintained partly by the state, the men being in some instances paid out of the treasury, but more frequently by an assignment of land to each man called a jaghire. They are thus remunerated at the expense of the Newars, who are the cultivators of the soil and were the original proprietors. Hence Nepaul is a warlike state, not merely from the natural disposition of its Ghorka conquerors, but from the inducements held out to them to become soldiers.

What would our grumbling agricultural population say to having soldiers billeted in each village, and living on the fat of the land? The Newars say, "Take away the army and give us free trade;" the farmers in England say, "Keep up the army and take away free trade."

The minister told us of out-stations at which different regiments were posted, and wanted us to believe that the standing army of Nepaul exceeded 25,000 men. Every male is obliged to serve in the army for a year, and it requires great interest to be allowed to remain above that period, so eagerly is the profession of arms sought after.

Immediately facing the parade-ground stands the famous monument built by Bheem Singh, one of the most eminent prime ministers that Nepaul has ever seen, and who has left behind him proofs of his greatness in the many works, both useful and ornamental, which he erected.

Two winged lions guard the chief bridge over the Bhagmutty, by which Katmandu is approached, and pronounce Bheem Singh its builder. Numerous temples and handsome palaces are adorned in like manner, but the monument above mentioned is the most remarkable memorial of his greatness, and is the chief ornament of the city. The people are deservedly proud of this its distinguishing mark, for, except as minarets, single columns are unknown in India, and in this respect their mountain capital can boldly challenge a comparison with the proudest city of the plains. The monument resembles in shape a portable telescope fully drawn out, and rears its head to a height of nearly 200 feet above the surrounding houses. The Minister Sahib contended that it was higher than the monument of London. This, as in duty bound, I patriotically denied; but which of us was led into error by partiality for our respective countries I am not prepared to say. The Mahila Sahib accompanied us to the summit, whence we had a most magnificent view. Looking down into the city beneath us, we could discern the turning of every narrow street, the palaces situated in the midst of gardens, the hovels in the midst of dunghills, though I am bound to say that the former preponderated in number, and the houses of the city were for the most part substantial and well built. Some of these streets were now crowded with a motley multitude, returning home from the review, the bright uniforms mixing amongst them as the soldiers joined their families after being dismissed parade, or here and there marched in companies back to the barracks. Officers were scampering down streets on ponies, dragging along the horse-boys, who were holding on by their tails. All this the Mahila Sahib pointed out with much affability. Had he been the man to seize a good opportunity, that was the moment to give Jung a push over the low parapet; but the Mahila Sahib is a man without decision of character; so we all descended, and he allowed the minister to reach the bottom his own way. We then proceeded with Jung to his residence, there to partake of a farewell feast. The carriage in which we were driving was one I had seen brought over the mountain passes on men's shoulders in detached portions; and this emanation from Long-Acre was to be trundled for the rest of its existence along the three or four miles of carriage-road which the valley of Nepaul can boast. Our way lay through narrow lanes, walled in by the enclosures of different rich men's suburban residences, and the prolific orange-trees drooped their luscious fruit over the garden walls for the benefit of any one who chose to pick them, as they hung temptingly over-head. Jung showed us his horticultural arrangements with no little pride. His house is situated in the midst of gardens, adorned with fountains and reservoirs, and he informed us that upon one aqueduct alone he had expended 30,000*l.* The garden was in its infancy, and, notwithstanding the great formality with which it was laid out, bid fair to do credit to Jung's taste and industry. In one direction the gardens extend to the river side, where he has built some handsome baths, not far distant from which, and at one corner of his grounds, stands a four-turreted building, inhabited by the Ranee of Lahore, who has taken refuge from the English under the hospitable roof of Jung Bahadoor. Here this extraordinary woman leads a secluded life, rarely venturing outside her doors, and never giving any one a chance of judging for themselves of her rumoured beauty. She is, no doubt, meditating some bold design worthy of the heroism she has proved herself to possess, for she is said still to retain hope where hope is surely forlorn.

We had not on this occasion walked a whole day over Nepaul roads, as was the case when last we dined with Jung; consequently, when his feast was set before us, we did not do justice to it. Perhaps our appetites were spoiled by the parting which was about to take place, for we were not to see his Excellency any more, and to part from the prime minister of Nepaul is not like parting from any other man. Even were he only a casual acquaintance, it would cause a different feeling from that of bidding adieu to one who was to lead a peaceable life, and in all probability die in his bed ; but when the chances are strongly against either of these suppositions, and when the friend whom you are leaving is a man of so interesting a character, the possessor of such great talents and of so many amiable qualities, one with whom you have journeyed and hunted and undergone all sorts of adventures and witnessed all sorts of scenes, and who has on all occasions proved himself a kind friend, an hospitable host, and an agreeable companion, it is anything but pleasant to look upon him for the last time. Doubtless, in the early years of his yet uncivilised life, Jung Bahadoor was guilty of great barbarities and crimes, but it was war to the knife, and self-defence no less than ambition prompted the acts of that bloody drama. Now he has proved himself a changed man, and his late generous and humane conduct might well read a useful lesson to many in the civilised societies in which he learnt to be what he now is, since he does not fear to change a line of conduct when its error is palpable.

The time at length arrived when we were compelled to bid adieu to this extraordinary man, whose future career is a matter of such vast importance to the country he rules with almost absolute power. Expressing the hope that the day might yet come when I should meet him in my own country, I took leave of my kind-hearted but perilously-situated entertainer as I would of a friend in a galloping consumption.

During my whole stay in Nepaul the weather had been unusually foggy, and the snowy range only displayed its wonders now and then. On the day following the review the sky was unclouded; I therefore resolved to ascend the Sheopoori, a mountain which rises to a height of 2000 feet above the valley, and from which it was said a most magnificent view of the snowy range is obtained. The ascent commenced at a distance of five miles from the Residency, and was very fatiguing from the total absence of any path, the steepness of some part of it, and the thick jungle through which we had to push our way. It occupied two hours' stiff climbing for one in pretty good mountain condition, but no fatigue seems too great if it is rewarded by a good view; and there is no prospect so cheering to the mountain traveller as that of an unclouded sky, with the summit of the hill he is ascending in clear relief against it.

At last we reached the shoulder, from whence I had a peep that made me long for more, but, determined not to spoil the effect, I pushed resolutely on after my guide through a low scrubby jungle, along a barely perceptible woodcutter's path, until the crisp snow crunching beneath our feet betokened our great elevation. I was glad to halt for a moment and cool my mouth with the snow, a luxury I had not experienced for years.

A few yards more and we gained the summit; a sort of shed, the residence of some departed holy man, marked the highest point, upwards of 6000 feet above the sea.

A keen sharp wind whistled about the ruin as I jumped on to a half broken down wall in order to look over the low bushes which surrounded me. From this position a panorama, in every respect as magnificent as it was wonderful, stretched itself, if I may so speak, as well above as below me. Northward, and not thirty miles distant, the Himalayas reared their heaven-piercing summits, peak succeeding peak, and crag succeeding crag, far as the eye could reach, from east to west a glittering chain, while here and there the light clouds which hung upon its rocks and precipices became thinned, till they vanished altogether, or, rising in denser masses from some dark valley, obscured the lower portions of the range, only to give relief to the summits and elevate them in appearance—an aid they little needed, for the height of the lowest level of the chain is upwards of 15,000 feet. But it was not the actual height of the various peaks, nor the masses of glistening snow which clothed them, brightly reflecting the rays of an almost vertical sun, and tinted by the most brilliant hues, that was the chief cause of wonder and admiration. It was the sharpness of the horizon-line against the serene clear sky which displayed precipices and crags of inconceivable grandeur, the overhanging peak looking down some thousands of feet upon the lower part of the range. Had it been possible to calculate upon such a stupendous scale, I felt I was gazing at sheer precipices 6000 or 8000 feet in depth, for the descent from 25,000 to 15,000 feet was not gradual, but the whole line was cragged and notched upon a scale of unsurpassable magnificence and grandeur.

The Dawalogiri, the highest mountain in the world, and 28,700 feet above the level of the sea, was as worthy a termination of the chain at one end as its rival, the Kinchin Jung, was at the other; while not ten leagues distant, and completely towering above me, the Gosain Than reared its gigantic head, the third highest in this mighty barrier.

Turning from this marvellous scene, I looked down upon the placid valley of Nepaul. Its four rivers appeared like silver threads, winding their way amidst rich cultivation to swell the waters of the parent Bhagmutty. Blooming and verdant, the populous plain lay embosomed in lofty mountains, shut out as it were from the cares of the world. It seemed a Paradise on earth, with an approach to heaven of its own along the summit of the Gosain Than.

I viewed with interest a country on which European foot had never trod, and my eye ranged over bleak hills enclosing fertile valleys, into which torrents first flung themselves wildly, then, flowing sedately through to the other end, dashed away again behind rocks and hills and jumbled masses of broken country, which must have afforded magnificent scenery as it gradually swelled into the towering mountains of the Emodus.

A distant hill was pointed out to me as that on which the city of Ghorka was perched, a fitting residence for the wild race to whom it gives birth. My guide also showed me the road to the mysterious capital of H'Lassa, winding through rocky glens, passable only for the droves of sheep that traverse those mountain defiles, a journey of twenty days in the Nepaul dominions; but how far from the frontier lay the city of the Grand Lama the guide did not know.

The valley of Noyakot is about eighteen miles distant from Katmandu, and was visited some years ago by Prince Waldemar of Prussia and his party. It does not offer much attraction to the traveller, and as I looked into it from the top of Sheopoori I thought it hardly worth the trip. Not so extensive as that in which Katmandu is situated, it lies lower and is very fertile. Its climate is much warmer and not so healthy.

Looking up the valley of Nepaul, I could distinguish at its farther end, twelve miles distant from the present capital, the ancient Newar city of Bhatgong, the second in importance in the days when Patn was the first. It has now fallen into much the same dismantled state as its old rival, while it looked much more picturesque, standing as it does on a commanding eminence, terraced with rich rice-fields. The Durbar is a fine old building, characteristic of the architecture of the country, and the town contains many ancient Newar buildings of much interest.

But the valley of Nepaul, and the wild mountains of Ghorka, and the dashing rivers and the rocky glens, all sank into insignificance when I returned once more irresistibly fascinated by the wonders which the snowy chain seemed to exhibit anew every moment, as clouds cleared away from off the frightful precipices, or laid bare huge craggy peaks. For an hour did I gaze upon this incomparable scene, as upon one which the experience of a lifetime can seldom boast, for, though I was prepared by an alpine experience in Europe, and had stretched my imagination to the utmost in my anticipations of what would be the appearance of the highest mountains in the world, I could never have conceived—far less is it possible for me to describe—the scene I beheld from the summit of Sheopoori.

CHAPTER XIV.

A visit to the Minister's brothers—Dexterity of Colonel Dhere Shum Shere—Scenes for lovers of the Fancy—Adieu to Nepaul—The view from the summit of the Chandernagiri pass—The scenery of Nepaul—The pass of Bhimphede—Night quarters.

It was out of the question my leaving Katmandu without paying a farewell visit to the Minister's two younger brothers, Juggut and Colonel Dhere Shum Shere, so I hurried over in the afternoon to their house, which was situated in the centre of the town. On my road I met them driving in a buggy, the only one of which the town could boast, and, as it is not considered *infra dig.* in Katmandu to go three in a gig, I jumped in between them, and we were soon tearing along the narrow street at a most reckless pace, and finally pulled up in a small square, where a great crowd seemed to be waiting for something to take place. A Katmandu crowd doubtless possesses the same instinct in this respect that crowds in civilized parts of the world do, and, as it proved, they were quite right in their expectations, for the exhibition which almost immediately followed was well worth seeing. The Colonel said he had something to show us, but we could perceive nothing out of the common except a huge bull buffalo, whose head was firmly lashed to a stake fixed in the court-yard so that it touched it from his forehead to his nose; he was then blindfolded, his legs were planted some distance apart, and he stood snorting at his confined position. Meantime we had jumped out of the buggy, the young Colonel, stripping himself of all superfluous clothing, had grasped a "korah," or native sword, and, first laying the keen edge of it gently upon the exposed neck of the buffalo, he drew himself to his full height, and raised his korah high above his head. Every muscle extended, every fibre strained, he seemed to concentrate his strength in a wonderful manner into that blow which was at one stroke to sever the extended neck of the buffalo. Down came the sword with sweeping force. I looked eagerly for the result; when suddenly his hand was arrested midway, and with a look of vexation the Colonel *let off the steam* he had got up for the occasion, as he pointed to one of the buffalo's legs; it had been moved an inch inwards, and that was sufficient to cause the failure of the operation. Three or four times did this occur, and it seemed essentially necessary to the success of the feat that the legs of the animal should be perfectly stationary in a particular position. How little was the buffalo aware that each movement he made prolonged his life some seconds! I could not help thinking that there was a strong resemblance between his position and that of Jung, for decidedly the only chance the Minister has of his life is to keep continually moving. At last down came the korah with crushing force, and passed right through the animal's neck : the headless trunk tottered for a second, and then fell heavily over.

I was horrified at seeing a second buffalo brought up for slaughter, and my horror was greatly increased when I understood that I was expected to exercise my skill upon it. This offer I declined as politely as I could, accepting from the young Colonel, as a remembrance of his dexterity and strength, the korah with which he had performed this extraordinary feat.

We next adjourned to another court-yard, which was surrounded with bulldogs and terriers of every description,—a collection worthy the most ardent votary of the Fancy. Two magnificent rams, which were tied up in the corners of the yard, soon after showed us that a sport existed in Nepaul unknown as yet to 'Bell's Life.' No sooner were these animals untied than they dashed at one another with the utmost fury ; the violence of the shock caused the combatants to recoil, and it was a matter of astonishment to us that their brains were not dashed out.

The whole fight consisted in their being separated and then let go at one another again. This continued without any apparent advantage on either side until we thought that they had inflicted punishment enough on one another for our amusement, and then they were both tied up, and left to meditate upon their splitting headaches and to scowl at one another across the yard.

We walked through the Colonel's house, and found in his drawing-room the usual collection of theatrical prints and portraits of opera-dancers, mixed up with those of old statesmen, which he seemed to think perfectly natural, and no doubt he fancies he has good reason for so thinking. There were also a piano and some European luxuries strangely mingled with barbarous inventions.

In leaving these two excellent young men, I bade adieu to the last of my fellow-travellers from Ceylon. My especial favourite of them all was Colonel Dhere Shum Shere, whose thoroughly frank and amiable disposition endeared him to every one, while his courage and daring commanded universal respect. I know of no one I would rather have by my side in a row than the young Colonel, and his brother Jung evidently thought so too when he chose him to assist in the capture of the conspirators in the attempt upon his life. Cheerful and lively, his merry laugh might be heard in the midst of a knot of his admirers, to whom he was relating some amusing anecdote, while his shrewd remarks were the result of keen observation, and proved his intellect to be by no means of a low order.

His elder brother Juggut was fat, lazy, and good tempered, but wanting the energy of his brothers. These two are the youngest members of the family, and are devotedly attached to Jung.

Mounting our ponies at an early hour on the following morning, we bade adieu to the Residency and its hospitable inmates, and cantered along narrow lanes bordered by hedges of prickly pear, and roughly paved with large stones : sometimes we passed between steep banks over gently swelling hills terraced to their summits, and reminding me strongly of a vine-growing country.

Soon the road became more broken, and, on gaining the top of a steep hill, we took our last view of the valley of Katmandu before commencing the ascent of the precipitous Chandernagiri. From this point we gazed with indescribable delight on the valley so peculiar if not unrivalled in its beauty : its compact red-brick villages or straggling houses, which, with their quaintly-carved gables, clustered up the hill sides ; its sacred groves containing numerous venerated shrines in picturesque proximity to the clear streams that gushed down from the neighbouring hills ; its ancient cities, whose dismantled walls enclosed the ruined tenements of a departed race ; the richly-cultivated knolls, the Chinese pagodas, the Bhuddist dagobas on the banks of the sacred Bhagmutty, the narrow but substantially-built brick bridges by which it was spanned, continually traversed by an industrious population ;—all these objects formed a picture, "with all the freshness and glory of a dream," to which the towering monument of Bheem Singh in the far distance, while it indicated the position of the capital of this favoured vale, was a fitting centre.

At Thankote, eight miles from Katmandu, we dismounted, and commenced in earnest the ascent of the Chandernagiri. It is the steepest pass on either of the roads by which the valley of Nepaul is entered, and for that reason seems generally chosen by the natives, who would not for the world miss the pleasure of toiling up an almost inaccessible mountain. They certainly cannot be accused of neglecting the opportunities their country affords them for strengthening the muscles of their legs. The traveller had need to have his shins cased if he intends to climb a hill with a Newar mountaineer, for the path is so steep that the hillmen, as they clamber up, frequently dislodge stones, which come tumbling down upon those behind. However, I should have despised the blows from the stones, and should not have cared for the fatigue of the rugged ascent, if, on reaching the summit of the Chandernagiri, I had been rewarded with the view which it commands in clear weather.

Colonel Kirkpatrick thus describes this glorious scene as it burst upon him in all its magnificence:—"From hence the eye not only expatiates on the waving valley of Nepaul, beautifully and thickly dotted with villages and abundantly chequered with rich fields fertilized by numerous meandering streams, but also embraces on every side a wide expanse of charming and diversified country. It is the landscape in front, however, that most powerfully attracts the attention—the scenery in this direction rising to an amphitheatre, and exhibiting to the delighted view the cities and numberless temples of the valley below, the stupendous mountain of Sheopoori, the still supertowering Jib Jibia, clothed to its snow-capped peak with pendulous forests, and finally the gigantic Himaleh, forming the majestic background to this wonderful and sublime picture."

This majestic background was now concealed behind a dense bank of clouds, and the prospect was bounded by Sheopoori.

The snowy range is the most striking feature in Nepaul scenery, and the most important element in its composition, since the effect produced by the grandeur of its stupendous summits is probably unequalled.

It would be hardly fair to compare the valley in which Katmandu is situated with any other part of the world, since it is so peculiar in its characteristics and totally unlike the rest of the Nepaul dominions ; but, standing on the summit of Chandernagiri, and looking over the mountainous district which stretched away to the south, and across which our road lay, we could not but be struck by the bleak appearance of the mountains, neither desolate nor rugged enough to possess the majesty of a bold and sublime solitude, nor sufficiently wooded and populous to exhibit that softer and more animating character which in the scenery of Switzerland is no less charming than its grandeur is imposing. Of course this does not apply to all Nepaul; the lower ranges are more woody, the valleys more sunny and fertile, but there is a lamentable want of water throughout. I do not remember ever to have seen so much as a horse-pond in Nepaul, or a single waterfall of any magnitude: the traveller will therefore probably be disappointed in the scenery, until he reaches the Chandernagiri, when indeed he must be difficult to please if he is not fascinated by the view of the valley at his feet, unsurpassed in the singular character of its beauty, and of the mountains beyond it, unparalleled by any in the whole world.

We followed the course of the stream down the mountain and along the valley of Chitlong, until we reached the foot of the Bhimphede pass, when, striking into the path by which we had entered Nepaul, we toiled up it, reaching the summit just before sunset, when we were delighted by the farewell view of the snowy mountains which we obtained at this point. The upper edge of the curtain of clouds had now become slightly lower, allowing a single peak to show itself. Gilded by the rays of the declining sun, it shone out in strong relief, like some unusual phenomenon; and as we gazed upon it high in the heavens we found it difficult to believe that it was part of the earth we stood on, and felt almost inclined to agree with the faithful, who throughout India regard this heaven-piercing summit as the centre of the universe, around which the sun, moon, and stars perform their courses, the sacred and mysterious Mount Menou.

Gradually the bright crimson rays of the setting sun began to fade, and reminded us that we had to make a long descent ere we could reach the tent pitched at the bottom for our reception; and our former experience had taught us that the Bhimphede pass was not the most pleasant road in the world on which to be benighted. So we hurried on at the risk of our necks, the loose stones rolling down before us, and rendering our footing anything but safe in the growing darkness.

When we reached the foot of the mountain our servants met us with torches and guided us to the tent; and as we spread our dinner upon a rickety old bedstead, which, wonderful to relate, this out-of-the-way village supplied, we came to the conclusion that there were many worse lodgings in the world than the snug little single-poled tent at the old Newar village of Bhimphede.

CHAPTER XV.

A dilemma at Bisoleah—Ignominious exit from the Nepaul dominions—The resources and capabilities of Nepaul—Articles of import from Thibet and Chinese Tartary—A vision of the future.

At Bhimphede we remounted our elephant, following, as before, the valley of the Rapti to Hetowra, thence through the great saul forest to Bisoleah, where we expected to find our palanquins. In this we were not disappointed; but unfortunately our bearers, tired of waiting for us at so uninteresting a spot, had thought themselves justified in absconding; which proceeding, while it was a considerable saving to us in a pecuniary point of view, was particularly annoying under existing circumstances, the day being far advanced and Segowly still thirty miles distant. However, by dint of a great deal of threatening, and coaxing, and bribing, and a very frequent use of the magic name of the Minister Sahib, who, we assured them, would take into his especial favour every coolie that volunteered for our service, and would visit with his heavy displeasure all those who refused, we induced a sufficient number of men to agree to bear our empty palanquins. Unloading two ponies, which were carrying cotton, we put our luggage on one, riding the other by turns, and so, one of us sitting on a rough sack without bridle or stirrups, the other walking by his side, we marched out of the village and across the open plain of the Terai. We were soon after left in darkness, and, becoming separated from our palanquins, as was to be expected, we lost our way, and wandered for some time disconsolately over the grassy plain, until at length, stumbling upon a village, we procured a guide and overtook the bearers a little beyond the Nepaul frontier. Ere we reached it, however, we were obliged to traverse numerous streams, which we crossed riding double on our pony. Altogether we made our exit from Nepaul in very different style from that in which we had entered it, and were not a little glad to arrive at Segowly shortly before dawn.

The journey from Katmandu to Segowly can scarcely be accomplished in less than three days and three nights, not on account of the distance, but of the frightfully bad roads, which quite preclude the possibility of travelling faster than at the rate of two miles an hour.

There is scarcely a country in the world in which the state of the roads is so much to be lamented, since, apart from the benefit which would accrue to Nepaul itself, we too should be gainers, by having not only the valuable productions of Nepaul brought to our markets, but also those of the more distant Thibet, which are always precious from their intrinsic value, and the cost of which is at present greatly increased by reason of the expensive journey across the Nepaulese hills in addition to the transit of the Himalayas.

The Terai is at present the only part of the Nepaul dominions which is profitable from the revenue yielded by its productions. Valuable timber and turpentine, ivory and hides, are shipped down the Boori Gundak, on which river Segowly is situated, to Calcutta; still the cost of a government license for cutting timber is so heavy as in a great measure to deter speculators from engaging in an undertaking in which so considerable an outlay is demanded, exclusive of the expenses attendant on the felling and transport of the timber. Besides the saul the Terai contains ebony, mimosa, and other useful trees.

The trade in hides is not, as I have already remarked, carried out to the extent it is capable of. But in spite of all these drawbacks, the Terai alone, of all the Nepaul dominions, can be looked upon by the British as offering a profitable field for trade and commercial speculations.

Nevertheless, the interior of Nepaul contains productions far more valuable than those of the Terai. Its mineral resources are such as would in all probability, if properly developed, render their mountainous, and in some parts barren country, one of the richest in the world. Iron, lead, copper, and zinc mines abound, and are in fact worked, but, from all I could learn, so very badly, that, even did their roads allow of the export of the metals, it is to be questioned whether, without the application of a better system, enough metal could be obtained to do more than supply the home demand.

However that may be, there is no doubt of the existence of these mines, and, if ever there were tolerable roads, the necessary skill for working them would doubtless follow. So backward are the Nepaulese in their treatment of minerals, that they cannot smelt lead : the fact of their *beating* cannon-balls into shape proves their incapacity to cast iron, unless it results from a peculiarity of the ore, so frequent in India, which, instead of yielding cast-iron at once when reduced in the usual way, gives wootz—a condition of iron closely allied to steel, ductile but not fusible. Of this I had no opportunity of judging.

Nepaul also possesses mines of sulphur, and, it is said, of antimony ; whether this latter is found in the country does not seem certain ; it is, however, an article of import from Thibet. Amongst other minerals are corundum, figure-stone, and talc ; and amongst the present exports from the interior of Nepaul may be noticed turmeric, wax, honey, resin, pepper, cardamums : all these, however, are exported in but small quantities, owing partly to the difficulty of transport, and partly to the want of enterprise and capital in a nation thoroughly ignorant of all mercantile transactions.

It is much to be regretted that no European is now allowed to settle in Nepaul; for its many latent resources must remain undiscovered, or at least undeveloped, until the present blind policy of its government is changed, when British enterprise and British capital introduces a new era in its commercial existence, which will doubtless prove no less profitable to the country itself than to the capitalist.

Of the immense expanse of country lying in a north-westerly direction towards Cashmere we know nothing, save by report, and that is not always to be trusted. The Minister told me that, in a province three days' journey from the capital in that direction, sufficient horses were bred to supply the wants of the whole country. That seemed perfectly possible, considering how limited is the demand in this respect; but, on our homeward journey, we passed a drove of upwards of two hundred long-backed spindle-legged colts, going up to Katmandu, and that did not seem exactly corroborative of the Minister's assertion.

But, whatever may be its capabilities as regards horses, it doubtless possesses many resources; but it is not on the productions of Nepaul alone that the European speculator would calculate, but on the rare and precious merchandise of Thibet and the northern provinces of China—such as the miledo, or exquisitely soft material fabricated from the wool of the celebrated shawl-goat, itself a rare and valuable animal; and the chowries or tails of a peculiar species of bullock inhabiting the snowy regions, at present an article of export from the hill states in the north-west provinces of India, and extensively used throughout the continent as fly-flappers.

Musk, procured from the musk-deer, is a most valuable article of commerce, and the present trade is exceedingly lucrative; of very inconsiderable bulk, and of great intrinsic worth, it is one of the few things that can be imported into India with a profit. It there fetches enormous prices; a small musk necklace, which I saw in the possession of the Minister, and which certainly was not a foot long, was valued at 25*l*. It is very seldom, however, that musk can be procured unadulterated. It is not, however, so much as an ornament, as a medicine, that we should use this now costly substance.

But the most valuable productions at present imported from Thibet are mineral. Immense quantities of salt are brought over the Himalayas on sheep's backs; gold-dust, borax, sulphur, antimony, arsenic, orpiment, and medicinal drugs are also imported into Nepaul.

The animals which abound in these cold regions, and which might be worth importing, are musk-deer, sheep, shawl-goats, chowrie bullocks, falcons, pheasants—in fact, it would be hopeless to attempt to enumerate all those productions, animal, vegetable, and mineral, which are now scarcely known except by name, but which will doubtless some day be objects of traffic and commercial enterprise. For instance, there are various medicinal drugs and dyes (among which may be mentioned madder and spikenard) which are said to exist, but are now almost totally unknown.

Among the present articles of import are embroideries, taffetas, chintz, silk, cotton, cloth, carpets, cutlery, sandalwood, tobacco, conch-shells, soap, &c.

Surely it is no very extravagant flight of imagination to suppose that the day may yet come when the unattainable and almost unknown productions of the trans-Himalayan regions will be transported across that mighty range, in well-appointed carriages, over macadamised mountain-passes; and the noble work of the scientific engineer will thus supersede the flocks of heavily-laden sheep, driven by uncivilized and ill-clothed Bootyas, who, "impelled by the force of circumstances over which they have no control," will don their smockfrocks and turn draymen; when the traveller, going to the coach-office, Durbar-square, Katmandu, may book himself in the royal mail through to H'Lassa, where, after a short residence at the Grand Lama Hotel, strongly recommended in Murray's 'Handbook for the Himalayas,' he may wrap himself in his fur bukkoo, and, taking his seat in a first-class carriage on the Asiatic Central Railway, whisk away to Pekin, having previously telegraphed home, *viâ* St. Petersburg, that he proposes returning through North America, and will, therefore, probably be detained a few hours longer than he had anticipated.

Such a state of things *we* may not live to see, but it is by no means unlikely that ere long a railway may run from Calcutta to the northern frontier of British India ; so that, when Nepaul is thrown open to European enterprise, its costly productions will be easily and cheaply transported to the nearest port, while the now almost uncivilized Nepaulese would obtain European luxuries unknown to any of them except Jung Bahadoor and his travelled suite.

Nor will the idea of a direct communication between Nepaul and Pekin seem either so improbable or impossible when we consider that an embassy now makes the journey once every five years. It occupies no less than two years, including a residence of less than two months in the capital of the Celestial Empire. I met two or three Nepaulese who had accomplished the enterprise, and who spoke in glowing terms of Pekin, and of the magnificence displayed throughout those portions of the Chinese Empire which they traversed, as well as of the great city of Lassa, and the terrible mountains to be crossed and the incredible dangers to be overcome.

The mission is composed of twenty-seven persons, and would not be admitted across the frontier of China if it consisted of one more or less than the stated number. It must arrive on the frontier on a certain day, and is subject to various rules and regulations : at the same time every provision is made by the Chinese for the comfort of the members of the embassy while on their journey. The journey from Pekin to Lassa has lately been made by Messrs. Huc and Gabet, two French Missionaries, and has been graphically described by them.

The Nepaulese look with the greatest awe upon their wealthy and highly-civilized neighbours; but the Minister, having now lived amongst people more warlike and accomplished than even the Chinese, regards them with great contempt; and I should not be surprised if, before long, accounts reach us of the invasion by the Nepaulese of the northern provinces of China, when the Minister would bring to bear his recently acquired knowledge, and would doubtless prove more than a match for the rudely-equipped forces of his Celestial Majesty. The Tartar race, however, who would oppose the progress of a Nepaul army, are a very different set from their tea-drinking countrymen on the southern coast.

But to return from Chinese Tartars to the

country we had just quitted. The kingdom of Nepaul extends for upwards of three hundred miles along the southern slopes of the Himalayas, and is said to contain a population of about five millions. Of these four hundred thousand inhabit the valley of Nepaul proper. The lands are divided into four classes of tenures—first, crown lands; secondly, Kroos or Soona Birtha, belonging to Brahmins or Newars; thirdly, Kohriya, or Bari, barren lands granted for cultivation; and, lastly (and this is the most extensive class of the four), Kaith, in which the proprietor is at all charges of tillage, dividing the produce with the cultivator.

The silver coinage of Nepaul is somewhat similar to that in use throughout British India; in all the northern provinces of which, adjoining Nepaul, it passes current: the copper coinage is most extensive, and consists of shapeless lumps of copper, eighteen or twenty of which go to a halfpenny; they are used by the natives of India in preference to their own pice.

But it is time to take leave of this interesting country, with its snowy mountains and sunny valleys—its ignorant people and enlightened Minister—its bloodstained past and hopeful future. I had already mentally whispered my adieu, as, riding behind my companion on the rawboned pony, I crossed the boundary stream; and pleased and interested as we had been with our short stay in Nepaul, still we could not help regretting that it had not fallen to our lot to discover new wonders—to encamp on the shores of the great lake situated in the distant province of Malebum, the existence of which was vaguely hinted at by my friend Colonel Dhere Shum Shere—to explore unvisited mountains, and to luxuriate in the magnificent scenery which they must contain; the enjoyment heightened by the feeling that we were the first Europeans who had penetrated their inhospitable recesses.

CHAPTER XVI.

Journey to Lucknow—Nocturnal disasters—View of the Himalayas—Wild-beast fights—Banquet given by the King of Oudh—Grand display of fireworks—Our return to cantonments.

UNQUESTIONABLY the pleasures of travelling cannot be said to be altogether unalloyed—a consideration which the journey from Segowly to Lucknow irresistibly forced upon our minds, how determined soever we might be to adhere to the traveller's first principle of making the best of everything. We left the station about dusk, upon a night in which the elements seemed to have combined to cause us as much discomfort as possible, and the violence of the storm about midnight compelled us to take shelter in every tope of trees we came to, or, as it appeared to me, wherever the bearers thought we stood a good chance of being struck by the lightning, which was vividly flashing in most unpleasant proximity. The deluge of rain soon made the path so slippery that our progress was much retarded, which would not have signified had it not happened that every now and then my slumbers were most disagreeably disturbed by a crash which flattened my nose against the side of the palanquin, or produced a violent shock to every part of my body, the effect of a slip of some unhappy bearer who was himself on the broad of his back, and had brought down the palanquin, bearers and all, in his tumble.

This occurred to me no less than five times in one night, and the consequence was that my palanquin was in even a worse condition than my body ; it did not possess a single uncracked panel, nor were there any means of keeping the doors in, far less closed, and the cooling influence of the rain which pelted upon me was only counteracted by the feverish anxiety I experienced from the momentary expectation of feeling the bottom give way, which would have inevitably landed me in the mud in a most deplorable condition—as had been the case with every book or other loose article about me.

Daylight, however, revealed a prospect which banished at once the remembrance of our nocturnal annoyances. The whole of the Himalayan range, tinged by the glowing rays of the rising sun, displayed to our delighted and astonished gaze its long and majestic line of snowy peaks, while the atmosphere, cleared by the night's heavy rain, brought out in bold relief the sharp outline of every point and angle from the clear horizon-line of the various summits down to where the light morning haze still shrouded their base.

Unobscured by intervening mountains, and

towering high above a sea of mist, well may they impress with wonder and admiration the traveller journeying over the plains of India, as he beholds them for the first time; nor could I, familiar as they were to me, withdraw my gaze until the increasing power of the sun rendered the atmosphere more hazy, and gradually veiled this glorious picture from my view, as if it were too precious to be exhibited for any length of time.

The journey to Goruckpore occupied us two nights and a day of incessant travelling over a flat but cheerful looking wheat country. It is a pretty little station, containing a regiment and a few civilians, and is situated on the banks of the Rapti, our old Nepaulese acquaintance under a very different face.

The Gograh, which we crossed the following morning, is the boundary that divides the British territory from that of his Majesty of Oudh; and Fyzabad was the first town in his dominions at which we halted. Situate about six miles from the river, it is approached by a narrow muddy lane which winds among numbers of squalid huts, while a considerable sprinkling of handsome mosques and minarets showed the predominance of Mahomedanism in the country in which we were now travelling; but they all seemed falling to decay, and were inhabited chiefly by Hindoo monkeys, who lazily inspected one another on the sunny corners of some ruined temple, or chased each other irreverently through the sacred groves.

Fyzabad was formerly the capital; but the seat of government was changed to Lucknow at the accession of Azof-up Dowlah in 1775.

We were not sorry, after spending another twenty-four hours in our rickety palanquins, to see the massive mosques and lofty minarets of Lucknow looming in the distance, while handsome buildings in varied styles of architecture gave to this city a handsome and more imposing appearance than any I had yet visited in the provinces of India.

We had been so much delayed by the weather, that we missed seeing the wild-beast fight, which was just concluded as we entered the town. This was not so much to be regretted, however, since, from all we heard, it had on this occasion proved a tame affair, though it is often most exciting. The fight between the buffalo and tiger seemed to have caused most interest, but the unfair practice of blunting the horns of the buffalo was not congenial to the fair-play feelings of the British portion of the community. Those who have witnessed a combat between a hyena and a donkey, however, say that it exceeds in its ludicrous interest any other of these animal encounters; the donkey (as is natural) possesses the sympathies of the spectators, and usually comes off victorious.

His Majesty had prepared a grand entertainment for the evening, whither, in company with my kind host, the Assistant Resident, I was by no means sorry to repair—for the King of Oudh is necessarily associated in one's mind with exquisite sauces and viands, and we promised ourselves a first-rate dinner after our tedious journey.

The street leading to the palace was brilliantly illuminated, as was also the palace itself, while the view from the reception-rooms was most unique. The glare of lamps lighted up a square, in which was a garden fitted with the grotesque frames of the various fireworks of the evening. Birds and beasts of all descriptions were there, waiting to be let off. Meantime, extraordinary equipages came driving up in rapid succession; the magnificent coach-and-six of the King was followed by the unpretending buggy of the bold subaltern, while natives of high degree descended from gorgeously attired elephants, or sprang lightly off their prancing Arabs: the varied costumes of the different guests as they passed under a blaze of lamps added not a little to the brilliancy and novelty of the scene.

The court-yard behind contained a large tank, in which the reflection of hundreds of lamps glittered brightly. Servitors, soldiers, and officers of his *Condimental* Majesty's household, filled every available portion of the yard. The spacious reception and banqueting rooms were crowded to excess, and smelt like a perfumer's shop in which, by some accident, all the bottles had been left uncorked; while brilliantly-attired natives scratched past you, glittering with jewels, and *chevaux de frise* of sharp gold tinsel.

At last the King made his appearance, and the guests all jostled into chairs as best they might. My position, almost immediately opposite his Majesty, afforded me ample opportunity of inspecting the quantity and quality of the jewels with which his person was absolutely loaded, and which I had never seen equalled in magnificence: a rope of pearls, passing over one shoulder, was tied in a knot at his waist, from which the costly ends negligently depended; his turban and breast were covered with diamonds and other precious stones; and it was a matter of wonder that he did not sink under the heat of the room, combined with the extent of mineral productions he carried on his person. But the jewels, though worthy of great attention, did not possess nearly so much interest in my eyes as did the mode by which he renovated the burly form that they adorned. On one side of him stood the bearer of his magnificently-jewelled hookah, on the other the bearer of the royal spoon, the contents of which he was already wistfully surveying as it was mixed up by the skilful feeder into the form and consistency that his Majesty loved, and put, as a nurse would put pap, into his Majesty's mouth, which was then carefully wiped by another man, who, I presume, is called the "wiper," and who was succeeded in his turn of duty by the hookah-bearer, who gently inserted the mouthpiece between the royal lips, in order that his Majesty might fill up, by a puff of the fragrant weed, the time required for the preparation of another spoonful. This routine of feeding, wiping, and smoking was only varied when the King slowly licked his lips, which he did in a dignified manner, and with a reproachful look at the wiper, whereat the wiper might be observed to tremble: poor wiper! I dare say that, if his Majesty finds it necessary to lick his lips thrice in one meal, it is equivalent to signing poor wiper's death-warrant. But his Majesty was not the only person that licked his lips; I found myself repeatedly doing the same, but it was with the feelings of a hungry hound as he envies a more fortunate member of the pack the possession of a juicy bone. Though the royal table groaned with viands, and though I was famishing, there was nothing but sponge-cake that any but a madly imprudent person could have ventured on. The cold cutlets, fried in rancid lard, rise up before me now, an unpleasant vision of the past; and I distinctly remember the mingled disgust and horror which I felt while breaking the crust of yellowish tallow to help a gallant young officer near me, who must have endured the privations of a Sutlej campaign to enable him to eat it.

At last we discovered some drinkable champagne, and drank her Majesty's health, with all the honours; after which we paid a similar compliment to his Majesty of Oudh, while all the grandees of the realm—who, sitting on chairs like ourselves, lined one side of the long range of tables, and seemed enveloped in a blaze of glistening jewels—looked as if they thought it all a very disrespectful proceeding.

There was a very loud band that played "God save the Queen," and two or three very discordant singing-women, who sang what I suppose was an Ode upon Sauce, as being the Oudh national anthem. At length dinner was over, and immediately there was a rush to the windows to see the fireworks, which seemed to be all let off at once, so that it was impossible to distinguish anything but a universal twisting and whirling, and fizzing and cracking; and an elephant looked very brilliant for a moment, and then went off through his eyes with a bang, and was no more;—sham men exploded; and real men jumped into sparkling, crackling flames; and rockets and fire-balloons went up; so that, if the lessee of Vauxhall or Cremorne could let off or send up half as many things as were let off and went up on this occasion in the court-yard of the Lucknow Durbar, he would make a fortune. At last everything that had not gone in some other direction went out; the King stood at the top of the stairs, and those who were presented, after receiving tinsel necklaces from the hands of royalty, passed down stairs, and the guests went away by whatever means of conveyance they might possess—a very motley and somewhat noisy party. The mode which we made use of to return to cantonments, a distance of four miles, was rather singular, not to be recommended except on an emergency: the carriages seemed to have decreased in proportion as the number of guests had multiplied, and in some unaccountable manner many of us were left to accomplish our return as best we could. It was in vain that we attempted to persuade the seven occupants of a buggy to receive us among them—we met with a stern refusal. It was useless to supplicate a number of rich Baboos, on a handsome elephant, to help us in our difficulties; the rich Baboos laughed, and told us we might get up behind, if we liked. And so all that brilliant throng went whirling back to cantonments, and we were left disconsolately standing in the court-yard, with the probability of having to trudge home. This was not to be thought of for a moment, and we had just arrived at a pitch of desperation when a handsome carriage, with the blinds all up, and drawn by a pair of high-stepping horses, came rattling toward us. Not a moment was to be lost; we rushed frantically forward and ordered an immediate halt. In vain did the venerable coachman and determined-looking servant intimate to us that the carriage was his Majesty's; his Majesty, we assured them, was still carousing in his palace; so depositing them both in the interior, without loss of time we mounted the box, and a moment after the high-stepping horses were dashing along the road to cantonments in brilliant style. We looked contemptuously down into the buggy, still clung to by its seven occupants, and galloped at a startling pace past the jocose Baboos, very much to the annoyance of their sedate elephant. On arriving at the cantonments we liberated his Majesty's domestics, and, ordering them to be careful how they heated his high-caste Arabs on their way back, we adjourned to a repast, to which the king's dinner had not incapacitated us from doing ample justice.

CHAPTER XVII.

A Lucknow Derby-day—Sights of the city—Grand Trunk Road to Delhi—Delhi—The Coutub—Agra—The fort and Taj—The ruins of Futtehpore Secreh—A loquacious cicerone—A visit to the fort of Gwalior—The Mahratta Durbar—Tiger-shooting on foot.

On the following morning, in spite of all this dissipation, we, as well as the greater part of the population of Lucknow, were perfectly ready to go to the races, which took place at an early hour. After seeing the first race, which was a well-contested one, and in which the natives seemed to take particular interest, I went towards the town, and was amused on the way by comparing the various conveyances used at Lucknow with those that may be seen on the road to Epsom on the Derby-day.

Here came dashing along a coach and six, the four leading horses ridden by postilions, while a sporting Baboo drove the wheelers, and two more sporting friends sat inside, and outriders vociferously cleared the way. Here two of the King's eunuchs jogged along in great style on camels with gaudy trappings; after them came prancing steeds bearing some gorgeously-dressed young princes, and then innumerable elephants bearing all sorts of disreputable-looking characters, the gents and blacklegs of the Lucknow community. In fact, I recognised specimens of nearly all the various classes of society which are to be met with at races in England, except that none of the fair sex were to be seen on this occasion.

There can be no doubt that Lucknow is a fast place, and contains a very sporting population ; and, if I remember right, the winning horse was the property of the turbaned owner of a four-in-hand.

As in duty bound, we explored the whole city, but a correct idea of the edifices with which it abounds is only to be gained from the drawings, which are executed by the natives with the most delicate minuteness, and convey a very correct notion of the exterior of the handsome mosques, minarets, tombs, and palaces, which render Lucknow a most interesting locality.

The Imaum Bara is said to contain the largest arched room in the world, a fact which we very much doubted. The " Gate of Constantinople " is handsome ; not so La Martinère, an attempt at an Italian villa, the figures on the roof of which look as much out of keeping with the rest of the edifice as the building itself looks out of place planted in the midst of paddy-fields ; it was erected by General Claude Martine, originally a French grenadier, and it is now, according to his express intentions, devoted to educational purposes.

One cannot but be struck by the singular taste of eastern potentates, who are so much more careful to provide a handsome place for their reception when dead than they are for their residence while alive. Were I the King of Oudh I should immediately move into the handsome tomb at present vacant, and leave directions to be buried in my palace.

A night's journey took us to Cawnpore, one of the largest and most disagreeable-looking stations in India. Here I resumed my acquaintance with the great trunk road under more favourable circumstances, and was not a little pleased to find how rapidly I was approaching Delhi. The carriage in which I travelled was a small palanquin on wheels, which one horse dragged along with ease; and as the stages were short, and the road very good, he was generally put into a hand-gallop at starting, and kept his pace up for the five or six miles allotted to him.

The great number of carts we passed confirmed me in thinking that this was the proper line for an experimental railway. The country is here well cultivated throughout; there is no water-carriage to contend against, and the present means of conveying goods is lamentably slow and expensive. The formation of the country affords every facility for the construction of a railway, being perfectly level throughout; whereas between Calcutta and Benares, the Raj-mahal hills have to be traversed; besides these many advantages, this line would be attended with a pecuniary saving to the Government, as the two or three military stations now on this road might be abolished.

The sights at Delhi are worth a visit, but are too well known to need description. In the centre of the town stands the Jumma Musjid, the St. Peter's of Mahomedans; its handsome domes and tapering minarets are built of red sandstone and white marble, a combination which is common in the edifices of this city, and which produces a most agreeable effect. From the summit of one of the minarets an extensive view is obtained.

The large and well-built city, containing 156,000 inhabitants, is enclosed by a wall, beyond which the country stretches away in appearance much like the Campagna at Rome. It is covered with ruins, which, with a few modern tombs scattered amongst prostrate slabs, give it a picturesque aspect. Through this Campagna we drove one day to see the Coutub. We passed the handsome tomb of Suftur Jung, and the mausoleums of many other worthies, the splendour of whose present resting-places betokened their former greatness. The Coutub is a tall column that is said to have been originally intended for a minaret, though the Hindoos claim it as having been erected before the Mahomedan invasion; however that may be, it is a singularly beautiful monument, and rises to a height of 260 feet. It was worth toiling up its narrow circular staircase to enjoy the view which the summit afforded of the country I had just traversed; the Jumma Musjid at Delhi was discernible in the distance, while immediately below lay the large camp of the Commander-in-Chief, the tents of which were pitched with great regularity, and looked dazzling white in the bright sun. After descending the column, I wandered awhile amidst the ruins at its foot, some of which looked very much as if they were of *Jain* origin,—and then returned to a desirable tomb, which the hospitable commissioner has converted into a delightful retreat from the noisy city.

I left Delhi with no little regret after an agreeable sojourn of a week, and rolled rapidly over the excellent road to Agra, so smooth that it was *irresistible* to the laziest horse, and 130 miles were easily accomplished in eighteen hours including stoppages.

Of Agra the passing traveller can say little, because its wonders are so inexhaustible and so interesting. The magnificent tomb at Secundra of that greatest of Mahomedan princes, Ackbar, must be left to the description already given by travellers of more leisure; so must the fort and the white marble palace which it contains, where dwelt the powerful Aurungzebe when he made Agra his capital. It was an endless source of interest to me to wander through the paved courts and under the marble columns of that glistening palace,—to look down upon the river, winding at the base of the lofty walls,—to descend into dark vaults in which were fountains and baths with water ever cool,—to creep yet lower, with a dim flickering light, into the execution chamber, and stand under the beam which had sustained the fair form of many a frail and faithless beauty,—to retreat from the stifling influence of its confined air, and return to inspect delicate little mosques, in which the Queen and her maidens used to perform their devotions, and which were as pure and chaste as the ladies were supposed to be.

The only other interesting relics in the fort are the renowned gates of Somnath, which are placed in the arsenal, and which need no description from my pen. But the greatest sight which Agra affords is the far-famed Taj Mahal: situated on the banks of the river, it is a conspicuous object from every quarter, and is as beautiful in its proportions when seen from a distance as in its details when more closely and minutely inspected: an unfailing source of gratification to the beholder, it well merits repeated visits. In its vastness, in its costly material, in its beautiful proportion, and in its delicacy of detail, it stands a noble monument of the talent which devised, and of the skill which executed it. It is said to have incessantly occupied 20,000 men for 22 years, and three million pounds sterling were expended upon it.

The intention of Shah Jehan, whose ashes it covers, was to have connected it by a marble bridge with a tomb exactly similar on the opposite side of the river, in which were to be interred the remains of his wife. This vast design he never lived to accomplish, and his son, who was of an economical turn of mind, did not consider the maternal ashes worth a further expenditure of three millions, and so Shah Jehan and his wife lie buried in one tomb, which may safely be pronounced the most magnificent in the world.

* * * * * *

I like the Indian system of starting on a journey after dinner. When other people are going to bed, you get into your comfortable palanquin, and wake up 30 miles from your companions of the previous evening, who are only beginning to rub their eyes, when you have already actively commenced the work of exploring the sights at your destination. Thus did I inspect the old city of Futtehpore Secreh under the guidance of Busreet Alee, a garrulous old man, and a perfect specimen of a cicerone, with whom I at once plunged into the most extensive ruins I had seen in India: cloisters, colonnades, domes, walls, kiosks, and turrets, heaped together in the utmost confusion, a mass of red sandstone, except when some white marble denoted a more sacred or interesting spot as it glistened in the beams of the rising sun.

Ackbar, the founder of the spacious palaces here situated, was an exception to the general rule of Eastern potentates, and his residence must have been even more magnificent than the handsome tomb of Secundra, in which his ashes repose. The legend regarding the reason for which Futtehpore Secreh was pitched upon by the monarch as his seat of government is somewhat singular. It seems that he had long desired a successor to perpetuate his great name, and rule over his vast dominions, the possession of most of which he owed to his own strong arm and fertile genius; it was therefore a great disappointment to him that the wished-for prince did not make his appearance. Ackbar accordingly consulted Shah Selim Shurstre upon this important subject, and Shah Selim Shurstre, who lived at Futtehpore Secreh, recommended a pilgrimage to Ajmeer, which was no sooner accomplished than Ackbar became the happy father of Jehan Giri. In gratitude for so eminent a service, and in order to have the benefit of such sage advice in future cases of emergency, Ackbar left Delhi, and fixed his residence at Futtehpore Secreh, which place possessed the further advantage of being more in the centre of his recent conquests. Notwithstanding his devotion to the holy man, Ackbar was a most unorthodox Mahomedan, as the figures of animals carved upon the pillars of the palace plainly testify. These figures were sadly mutilated by his undutiful grandson, the bigoted Aurungzebe, who held all such representations in much the same horror that a Presbyterian would a picture of the Virgin.

Busreet and I went over the ladies' apartments, which must have been very cheerless, since they are entirely composed of immense slabs of red sandstone, and look hard and uncomfortable. Descending from them to the level of the court-yard, Busreet took me into a narrow sort of corridor, and jabbered incessantly for some minutes. I thought I could distinguish the words "hide and seek;" but it was so very unnatural to suppose that the only words of English Busreet knew were "hide and seek," that I imagined he was repeating some Hindostanee phrase, until he dodged round corners and behind pillars, crying out as he did so, "Hide and seek! Hide and seek!"—from which I at last understood that he meant to inform me that the ladies used to play that Occidental game in Ackbar's harem; so, after a short game to show the old man that I understood him, we strolled on to a singular kiosk-like little building, my guide every now and then renewing the game and hobbling round corners despite of my remonstrances to the contrary. The little temple was the residence of the holy man, and near it a room of most extraordinary construction astonished me not a little, since I could not divine its use, and Busreet afforded no information on the subject, as he pulled my head down and whispered something in my ear, which left me in doubt whether what he told me was a secret, or whether he meant to intimate that it was a whispering gallery: its real use I afterwards discovered.

In the centre of a square room was a pillar 15 or 16 feet in height, the circular top of which was six or eight feet in diameter and had been surrounded by a stone parapet; communicating with this singular pulpit-like seat were four narrow stone passages or bridges, one from each corner of the room. In each corner a minister of the realm used to sit, only one of whom might approach their royal master at a time. Seated on this centre point high above the heads of his subjects, who crowded the room below, and approached only by the four narrow causeways, the King deemed himself secure from assassination.

It was an original idea, and, after inventing so novel a method for guarding against treachery, he deserved to die in his bed, as in fact he did.

Emerging from this singular apartment, we crossed a square, in the midst of which was placed an immense slab of stone, raised a little off the ground; on each of the four sides of this slab there were 16 squares marked on the ground like those on a chess-board.

Four ladies used to stand on the squares on each division, making sixteen in all, each party of four dressed in garments of different colour from those worn by the others. The King and his ministers sat on the slab in the middle, and the game, which was something like chess, commenced. It must have been a glorious game: the prizes were numerous and worth playing for, and one can easily imagine the crafty old King moving his Queen so as to take the lovely slave of one of his ministers, or a handsome and fashionable young noble giving check to Queen and concubine; probably the Queen could not be taken, but it must have added immensely to the interest of the game to be playing with pieces that were interested in the result.

We ascended a handsome gateway of the mosque, 120 feet in height, whence I looked over a wide expanse of level country, while the intricate maze of ruins through which we had been wandering lay spread at our feet like a map; the wall of the city is still entire, and encloses a space of six miles in circumference, the extent of this once famous place.

The court-yard of the mosque, which was at least 150 yards square, contains the white marble tomb of the holy man. It is, without exception, the most perfect little bijou imaginable. The walls are composed of immense slabs, or rather screens of marble, delicately carved and perforated, so that, while they allow a dim light to penetrate, the effect of the tracery, when viewed from the interior, is exquisite. While I was admiring this beautiful structure Busreet suddenly assured me that he was very fond of tea. As he had already made many other observations equally unconnected with the matter in hand, I merely assured him of my sympathy; when the more home-question of whether I had any tea at once enlightened me as to his meaning. I accordingly invited him to take tea with me, and we sat on the steps of the good man's tomb, and had a sociable cup together; after which I entered my palanquin, and, travelling through the heat of the day, returned to Agra in a semi-grilled condition.

* * * * *

Having seen most of the sights of Agra (and it has a goodly share of its own), and having made the necessary preparations for the conveyance to Bombay of our party, now four in number, we took our departure from the handsome and hospitable residence of the Lieutenant-Governor, on the evening of the 9th of March, and drove in our buggies by moonlight over rather a wild country, in rather a wild manner, arriving at the station, where our palanquins were to meet us, a little before midnight.

An Indian coolie's powers of endurance are marvellous. Our cortège consisted of 112; and they were to carry ourselves, servant, baggage, and provisions, at the rate of thirty-five miles a night, for as many consecutive nights as we should choose to require their services.

We arrived at Dholpoor next day—looked down a magnificent well, about sixty feet in diameter, with corridors round it, and a handsome flight of stairs leading down to them—and then pushed on for Gwalior, crossing the battle-field of Maharajpore, and paying a visit to the fort perched upon the scarped rock. Some portions of the fort walls were covered with various devices in green and yellow porcelain, which added to their singular and characteristic appearance.

We visited the young Rajah in Durbar, and the difference between the Mahratta and Nepaulese Courts was most striking. The waving plumes, hussar jackets, and gold-laced pantaloons of the latter were exchanged for the simple white turban and flowing robe of the Indian senator; but though the character of their costume may have been more in accordance with our ideas of Oriental habits, there was a lamentable deficiency of intellect in their faces, and the fire and intelligence which flashed from the eye of the Highland noble were wanting in that of the Mahratta chief. After two days' agreeable sojourn at the Residency we proceeded for two or three consecutive nights over flat a dreary country, spending the days in the miserable little resthouses provided for the accommodation of the traveller, and generally picking up a few partridges for breakfast.

At Goonah we had a prospect of more important game. We here fell in with a most ardent sportsman : the numerous trophies of bears and tigers with which his bungalow was adorned proved his success as well as his skill.

With him we sallied forth at about 10 A.M., some on horseback and some on an elephant, all equally indifferent to the sun, fiercely blazing in an unclouded sky, and reached a dell, the sides of which were covered with a low scrubby jungle, where sport was to be expected.

As tiger-shooting on foot is almost unheard of in the northern part of India, and is practised in the southern only, because the tiger there is a much less formidable animal than his majesty of Bengal, we were told to proceed with considerable caution by the veteran, who posted us in the most likely places, saying to one of our party, as he stationed him in the most *favourable* locality, "I put you here because the tiger is nearly sure to charge down this hill ; and if he does, there will be very little chance of escape for you, as you see he has so much the advantage of you, that if you do not kill him with either barrel—and the skull of a tiger is so narrow that it is exceedingly improbable you will be able to do so—he must kill you ; but I would not for the world that you should miss the sport."

Thus did this self-denying Nimrod debar himself the pleasure of being charged by a tiger, reserving it, in the kindest manner, for his guests, who but half appreciated the sacrifice he was making on their account, from their dread of themselves becoming a sacrifice to the tiger. And as they crouched behind their respective bushes they had time to brood over the appalling stories of hairbreadth escapes just recounted to them by the gallant captain, who had been particular in describing the requisites for the successful tiger-shot—the steady hand and steady nerve—admitting that these were not always efficacious, as the last tiger he had encountered had struck him on the leg, and his torn inexpressibles existed to this day to testify to it. The thoughts of this and sundry other escapes he had experienced made the blood run cold, as one imagined every rustle of the leaves to be a bristling tiger, preparing for his fatal spring.

Gradually the beaters approached nearer and nearer, and, as the circle became smaller, peafowl innumerable flew over our heads with a loud whirr, their brilliant plumage glancing in the sunshine like shot-silk. A few moments more, and I perceived stripes gliding rapidly behind a bush, and a shot from L—— made me suspect that our *worst* anticipations had been realised, and that we had really found a tiger—a suspicion which soon disappeared, however, as a grisly hyæna bounded away, having received a ball in his hind-quarters, which unfortunately did not prevent his retreat.

The beaters soon after appeared over the brow of the hill, and relieved us for the present from further apprehension of that charge which was to seal our fate, for the monarch of the Indian jungle had changed his location. We beat some more jungles, in the hope of finding other game, but only succeeded in bagging a deer. I had a long shot at a four-horned buck, but the smooth bore of my piece was not equal to the distance.

On our way home we came upon a cave, which, from marks in the neighbourhood, bore evident signs of containing a panther; we accordingly attempted to smoke him out by lighting quantities of straw at the mouth, but he was not to be forced out of his secure retreat, and preferred bearing an amount of smoke that would have stifled a German student.

On the following day we renewed our attempt to find a tiger, and were to a certain extent successful, as at one time we were within a few yards of him, and could see the bushes move, but he succeeded in breaking through the line of beaters; and some deer and a neelgye were all the game we could boast of, notwithstanding a perseverance and endurance of heat worthy of greater success.

CHAPTER XVIII.

The carnival at Indore—Extraordinary scene in the palace of the Holkar—A night at the caves of Ajunta—The caves of Ellora and fortress of Doulatabad—The merits of a palkee—Reflections on the journey from Agra to Bombay—Adieu to India.

After a few days' more travelling over the hot dry plains of Malwa we reached its capital, Indore, where we spent some days at the hospitable mansion of the Resident, and paid a visit to the Rajah, whose palace is situated in the centre of that large and populous town. During our visit a most extraordinary scene occurred. It happened that a sort of carnival was going on; but the bonbons and bouquets of Italy are here represented by little balls containing red, purple, or yellow dust, which burst the moment they strike the object at which they are thrown, and very soon after the *row* commences two-thirds of the population are so covered with red dust that they present the most extraordinary appearance; but it is not the dust-balls which contribute so much to the dyeing of the population as the squirts full of similar coloured liquids, which are to be seen playing in every direction. Woe to the luckless individual who incautiously exhibits himself in the streets of Indore during the "Hoolie;" not that we ran any risk upon the occasion of our visit to the Rajah, as we were on that account tabooed, and could laugh at our ease at the rest of the claret-coloured world. Here a woman passed spotted like a coach-dog: she had just come in for a spent discharge, and had escaped the deluge, which her puce-coloured little boy had received so fully that his whole face and person seemed to partake of the prevailing tint; while yonder old grey-beard is dusting his moustache from the red powder which tinges it in strong contrast to the rest of his sallow countenance.

After going through the ceremony of squatting on the floor of the Durbar—our seven pair of unruly legs all converging to a common centre, from our inability to double them under us, as his Majesty did—we adjourned to the hall below to witness the "Hoolie" in safety. On each side of the court-yard was a sort of garden-engine, one filled with a purple and the other with a light-red fluid. The King's body-guard were now marched in and divided into two parties, each sitting under one of the garden engines. At the main gateway of the court-yard stood two elephants, with tubs of coloured liquid before them. At a given signal the gallant troops were exposed to a most murderous cross-fire, which they were not allowed to return: both garden-engines began playing upon them furiously, and the elephants, filling their trunks, sent the contents far and wide over the victims, who crouched down and bore in patience the blood-red storm. At the same moment that a dexterously-applied squirt whisked off some individual's turban, a fountain from the other side playing into his eyes and mouth prevented him from recovering it until some more fortunate neighbour, suffering perhaps from ear-ache, received the claret-coloured salvo with such violence that, if it failed to drive away the pain altogether, it must have rendered him a martyr to that complaint for the rest of his life.

After getting a thorough soaking they were sprinkled all over with a fine red powder, which, caking upon them, completed the ceremony by rendering them the most muddy, sticky-looking objects imaginable, as they withdrew from the presence of the young Rajah, after receiving pawn.

We were now offered balls of powder: had we thrown one at his Majesty, which some of his household seemed very anxious we should do, nothing could have saved us from a deluge. To commence the game upon the royal platform is the signal of indiscriminate warfare throughout the whole palace; the now passive troops would then have been allowed to retaliate, the garden-engines would have been stormed and captured by opposing squadrons, and the battle would have raged furiously until dark: whereas now, company of soldiers after company were ordered in to be shot down like sheep. We, however, were contented with seeing each party come in white and go out red, without wishing to go out red ourselves; besides which, we should have been outnumbered, and Britons, for the first time, would have been obliged to beat a retreat with tarnished honour as well as tarnished jackets.

The usual ceremony of presenting scents, spices, and garlands, having terminated, we left the young King, much pleased with his intelligence and good-nature; though only seventeen, he is a stranger to those vices which are generally inherent in natives, and inseparable from their courts.

* * * * *

We were ten days on our journey to the caves of Ajunta, having spent two or three at the hill fort of Aseerghur, a characteristic Mahratta stronghold; it is perched 700 feet above the plain, and just capacious enough to contain a regiment, who must find some difficulty in climbing its rocky steep approach, up which, however, the ponies of the garrison scramble nimbly enough.

We galloped over one afternoon from Furdapore to the caves of Ajunta, and were delighted with their romantic situation high up the rocky glen terminating in a waterfall, and so narrow, gloomy and silent, that it harmonized well with these mysterious caverns, in one of which, more free than the rest from bats, we determined to pass the night; and here, surrounded by staring Bhuddas and rampant elephants, and gods and goddesses making vehement love, according to the custom of such gentry, we had a most comfortable tea preparatory to turning in: spreading my blanket under the nose of a huge seated figure of Bhood, and guarded by two very tall individuals in faded painting, which, as they had watched over Bhood for twenty centuries, must have been well competent to perform the same kind office for me, I was soon comfortably asleep, my head pillowed on a prostrate little goddess, whom I was very reluctant to leave when daylight warned us to proceed upon the work of examining the wonders of the Rock Temples of Ajunta.

So much has already been written on the interesting subject of the caves of Ajunta, that they are more or less familiar to every one, or, if not already familiar, are destined soon to become so, thanks to the skill and energy of Captain Gill, who is at present engaged in making copies of all the paintings. These will form a splendid collection, and some of them have already been sent to England, and placed in the collection at the East India House. It was doubly delightful to us, who had just previously examined the originals, to look over the portfolios of this talented draftsman.

Ere we left the village of Ajunta we visited

its neat whitewashed mosque: the association connected with it must be replete with interest to the Englishman, when he calls to mind that in it the Duke of Wellington—then Sir Arthur Wellesley—wrote his despatches immediately previous and subsequent to the victory of Assaye.

The caves of Ellora are two days' journey from those of Ajunta, and are much more cheerfully situated on the face of a hill commanding an extensive view over a more smiling country than is usually to be met with in the Deccan.

It is difficult to say which set of caves are most worth seeing; differing in many respects, they may be said to afford equal attraction to the traveller. Ellora can boast of the wonderful "Kylas;" Ajunta of those most interesting frescoes which carry the art of painting back to an unknown period, but which at Ellora have been almost totally obliterated by the ruthless and fanatical zeal of Aurungzebe.

A few miles from the caves of Ellora frowns the rock fortress of Doulatabad, a conspicuous object from every side, and we soon discovered its interior to be as singularly interesting as its exterior was formidable and imposing. The rock itself is a pyramid rising abruptly to a height of 700 feet above the village which nestles at its base, while it is scarped all round to the broad moat by which it is encircled, forming a sheer precipice of 100 or 150 feet in depth.

Passing through a massive gateway which led into the town, we entered the fort by a similar approach, and crossing the moat by a narrow bridge we plunged into a dark hole directly opposite; then passing by torchlight through some small caves which were entered by very low portals, we began to ascend the inclined plane which wound up the interior of the rock, and which gradually became steeper till it ended in a flight of steps, our guides lighting us on our uncertain path, until we emerged into daylight by a large iron trap-door, pierced with innumerable small holes, the object of which, as well as of a groove in the rock communicating with the subterranean passage, was to enable the garrison, by filling the passage with smoke and flame, to suffocate and blind the besiegers should they ever succeed by any accident in penetrating thus far—in itself, as it seemed to me, a very improbable contingency. We clambered up the face of the rock to its summit, whence we had an extensive view of the arid plains of the Deccan.

Arungabad is the first station which we had visited in the dominions of the Nizam. We were now approaching the confines of civilization, and it became necessary to part with our palkees and the bearers, who had accompanied us from Agra. A separation from the latter was easily borne, and they, on their part, were no doubt glad to get rid of the burdens they had been carrying for the last month. But to bid adieu for ever to one's palkee is a severe trial; and no wonder, for to a man not in a hurry it is the most luxurious and independent means of travelling conceivable.

If judiciously arranged it contains everything the traveller can want—a library, a cellar, a soda-water range, a wardrobe, a kitchen; in fact, there is no limit to the elasticity of a palkee. My plan was, surreptitiously, to add a new comfort every day, and the unsuspecting coolies carried me along as briskly as if my palkee contained nothing but myself, and never seemed to feel the additional weight, upon the principle of the man who could lift an ox by dint of doing so every morning from the time when it was a calf.

Then the delightful feeling of security, and the certainty that your bearers won't shy, or come into collision, or go off the rails, or otherwise injure your nerves or bones. You are independent of hotels and hospitality. If the traveller in India depended upon the former, he would pass many a night with the kerbstone for his pillow, if he had not courage to claim the latter—which, be it remembered, he is certain to receive abundantly at the hands of the Burra Sahib. A modest man has his palkee; and for lack of courage on the one hand, and a resthouse on the other, he orders himself to be set down for the night by the wayside, and, shutting the doors towards the road, after boiling the water and making tea with the apparatus contained in his pantry, he lights his lamp, reads for an hour, pulls a light shawl over him, turns round, and goes to sleep as soundly as if he were sumptuously couched in Belgravia.

If the palkee be a good one, it defies weather ; but I admit it is not pleasant, on a dark night, to be carried along a slippery road with a careless set of bearers.

During the whole period of our journey since we had left Agra, with one or two breaks in its ordinary routine, we seemed to have been passing a monotonous existence at the same small and uncomfortable bungalow. It consists of two rooms ; in front is a tope of trees ; behind are a few low sandstone or trap hills, some scrubby bushes climbing up the sides, out of which a partridge may easily be flushed ; for the rest, the view extends over a boundless plain, assuming during the heat of the day a light yellow colour, at which period the coolies are all asleep in the verandah, snoring in an infinite and interesting variety of notes and keys.

At sunset we take a constitutional, followed by our portable residences, into which, after a romantic tea-drinking by the roadside, we turn in for the night, awaking at daylight to find ourselves thirty miles nearer to our journey's end, in a bungalow precisely similar to the one we had lately quitted, and containing the same rickety table, greasy with the unwiped remains of the last traveller's meal, which the book will inform you was eaten a month ago—the same treacherous chairs, which look sound until you inadvertently sit upon them—the same doubtful-looking couch, from which the same interesting round little specimens emerge, much to the discomfort of the occupant—the same filthy bath-room, which it is evident the traveller a month ago did not use—the identical old kitmutgar or bungalow-keeper, who looks as uncivilized as the bungalow itself, and seems to partake of its rickety and dirty nature—the same clump of trees before, and the same desert plain behind; —all tend to induce the belief either that you have never left the bungalow in which you spent the previous day, or that some evil genius has transported the said bungalow thirty miles for the express purpose of persecuting you with its horrors and miserable accommodation.

Thus are 700 miles insensibly accomplished in a month by the traveller, who only passes a dreamy existence in dâk bungalows, to be roused into violent action on his arrival at some sporting vicinity, a large cantonment, a native Court, rock temples, or other excitements, which must occur in the experiences of the Indian traveller.

I went seventy miles in a bullock hackery, the most unpleasant mode of travelling I conceive that can exist; then one hundred miles in a rickety phaëton with a pair of horses, which was in a slight degree less intolerable; and after visiting Mahabuleshwa, the hill station of Bombay, I reached that mercantile emporium itself, not a little pleased at seeing the sea on the English side of India. I was disappointed with the far-famed Bay ; but perhaps it is difficult to do justice to scenery after so much wandering, when the most interesting view is the sight of home. Certainly one's impressions of a place are regulated in a great degree by the circumstances under which it is visited. Had Bombay been the port of debarkation instead of embarkation, the bay would have been lovely and the various points of view enchanting; as it was, the prettiest object to my perverted vision was the "Malta" getting up her steam to paddle me away from that land, whose marble tombs and rock-cut temples will continue to afford attractions to the traveller when its Princes no longer exist sumptuously to entertain them, and whose towering mountains will still disclose fresh wonders when that last independent state which now extends along their base shall have been absorbed into one vast empire.

MISCELLANEOUS WORKS.

APPLETON'S Library Manual. 8vo. Half bound, $1 25.

——— Southern and Western Traveller's Guide. With colored Maps. 18mo. $1.

——— Northern and Eastern Traveller's Guide. Twenty-four Maps. 18mo. $1 25.

——— New and Complete United States Guide-Book for Travellers. Numerous Maps. 18mo. $2.

——— New-York City and Vicinity Guide. Maps. 38 cts.

——— New-York City Map, for Pocket. 12 cts.

AGNELL'S Book of Chess. A complete Guide to the Game. With Illustrations by R. W. Weir. 12mo. $1 25.

ANDERSON, WM. Practical Mercantile Correspondence. 12mo. $1.

ARNOLD, Dr. Miscellaneous Works. 8vo. $2.

——— History of Rome. New Edition. 1 vol., 8vo. $3.

——— History of the Later Roman Commonwealth. 8vo. $2 50.

——— Lectures on Modern History. Edited by Prof. Reed. $1 25.

——— Life and Correspondence. By the Rev. A. P. Stanley. 2d Edition. 8vo. $2.

AMELIA'S Poems. 1 vol., 12mo. Cloth, $1 25; gilt edges, $1 50.

ANSTED'S Gold-Seeker's Manual. 12mo. Paper, 25 cts.

BOWEN, E. United States Post-Office Guide. Map. 8vo. Paper, $1; cloth, $1 25.

BROOKS' Four Months among the Gold-Finders in California. 25 cts.

BRYANT'S What I Saw in California. With Map. 12mo. $1 25.

BROWNELL'S Poems. 12mo. 75 c.

CALIFORNIA Guide-Book. Embracing Fremont and Emory's Travels in California. 8vo. Map. Paper, 50 cts.

CARLYLE'S Life of Frederick Schiller. 12mo. Paper, 50 cts.; cloth, 75 cts.

CHAPMAN'S Instructions to Young Marksmen on the Improved American Rifle. 16mo. Illustrated. $1 25.

COOLEY, A. J. The Book of Useful Knowledge. Containing 6,000 Practical Receipts in all branches of Arts, Manufactures, and Trades. 8vo. Illustrated. $1 25.

COOLEY, J. E. The American in Egypt. 8vo. Illustrated. $2.

COIT, Dr. History of Puritanism. 12mo. $1.

CORNWALL, N. E. Music as It Was, and as It Is. 12mo. 63 cts.

COUSIN'S Course of Modern Philosophy. Translated by Wight. 2 Vols., 12mo. $3.

COGGESHALL'S Voyages to Various Parts of the World. Illus. $1 25.

DON QUIXOTTE DE LA MANCHA. With 18 Steel Engravings. 16mo. Cloth, $1 50.

EMORY'S Notes of Travels in California. 8vo. Paper, 25 cts.

ELLIS, Mrs. Women of England. 12mo. 50 cts.

——— Hearts and Homes; or Social Distinctions. A Story. Two Parts. 8vo. Paper, $1; cloth, $1 50.

EVELYN'S Life of Mrs. Godolphin. Edited by the Bishop of Oxford. 16mo. Cloth, 50 cts.; paper, 38 cts.

FAY, T. S. Ulric; or, The Voices. 12mo. 75 cts.

FOSTER'S Essays on Christian Morals. 18mo. 50 cts.

FREMONT'S Exploring Expedition to Oregon and California. 25 cts.

FROST, Prof. Travels in Africa. 12mo. Illustrated. $1.

FALKNER'S Farmer's Manual. 12mo. 50 cts.

GARLAND'S Life of John Randolph. 2 Vols., 12mo. Portraits, $2 50.

GILFILLAN, GEO. Gallery of Literary Portraits. Second Series. 12mo. Paper, 75 cts.; cloth, $1.

——— The Bards of the Bible. 12mo. Cloth, 50 cts.

GOLDSMITH'S Vicar of Wakefield. 12mo. Illustrated. 75 cts.

GOULD, E. S. "The Very Age." A Comedy. 18mo. Paper, 38 cts.

GRANT'S Memoirs of An American Lady. 12mo. Cloth, 75 cts.; paper, 50 cts.

GUIZOT'S Democracy in France. 12mo. Paper cover, 25 cts.

——— History of Civilization. 4 Vols. Cloth, $3 50.

——— History of the English Revolution of 1640. Cloth, $1 25.

HULL, Gen. Civil and Military Life. Edited by J. F. Clarke. 8vo. $2.

HOBSON. My Uncle Hobson and I. 12mo. 75 cts.

GOETHE'S IPHIGENIA IN TAURIS. A Drama in Five Acts. From the German by G. J. Adler. 12mo. 75 cts.

KAVANAGH, JULIA. Women of Christianity, exemplary for Piety and Charity. 12mo. Cloth, 75 cts.

KENNY'S Manual of Chess. 18mo. 38 cents.

KOHLRAUSCH'S Complete History of Germany. 8vo. $1 50.

KIP'S Christmas Holidays at Rome. 12mo. $1.

LAMB, CHAS. Final Memorials. Edited by Talfourd. 12mo. 75 cts.

LAMARTINE'S Confidential Disclosures; or, Memoirs of My Youth. 50 c.

MISCELLANEOUS WORKS—Continued.

LEE, E. B. Life of Jean Paul F. Richter. 12mo. $1 25.

LEGER'S History of Animal Magnetism. 12mo. $1.

LETTERS FROM THREE CONTINENTS. By E. M. Ward. 12mo. Cloth, $1.

LORD, W. W. Poems. 12mo. 75 c.

——— Christ in Hades. 12mo. 75 cts.

MACKINTOSH, M. J. Woman in America. Cloth, 62 cts.; paper, 38 cts.

MAHON'S (Lord) History of England. Edited by Prof. Reed. 2 Vols., 8vo. $4.

MICHELET'S History of France. 2 Vols., 8vo. $3 50.

——— Life of Martin Luther. 12mo. 75 cts.

——— History of Roman Republic. 12mo. $1.

——— The People. 12mo. Cloth, 63 cts.; paper, 38 cts.

MATTHEWS & YOUNG. Whist and Short Whist. 18mo. Cloth, gilt, 45 cts.

MILES on the Horse's Foot; How to Keep it Sound. 12mo. Cuts. 25 cts.

MILTON'S Paradise Lost. 38 cts.

MOORE, C. C. Life of George Castriot, King of Albania. 12mo. Cloth, $1.

NAPOLEON, Life of, from the French of Laurent de l'Ardeche. 2 Vols. in 1. 8vo. 500 Cuts. Im. mor., $3.

OATES, GEO. Tables of Sterling Exchange, from £1 to £10,000—from 1-8th of one per cent. to twelve and a half per cent., by eighths, etc., etc. 8vo. $3.

——— Interest Tables at 6 per cent. per Annum. 8vo. $2.

——— Abridged Edit. $1 25.

——— Interest Tables at 7 per cent. per Annum. 8vo. $2.

——— Abridged Edit. $1 25.

——— Sterling Interest Tables at 5 per cent. per Annum, from £1 to £10,000. 4to. $5.

O'CALLAGHAN'S History of New-York under the Dutch. 2 Vols. $5.

POWELL'S Living Authors of England. 12mo. $1.

REPUBLIC OF THE UNITED STATES; Its Duties, &c. 12mo. $1.

REID'S New English Dictionary, with Derivations. 12mo. $1.

RICHARDSON on Dogs. Their History, Treatment, &c. Cuts. 25 cts.

ROBINSON CRUSOE. Only complete Edition. 300 Cuts. 8vo. $1 50.

ROWAN'S History of the French Revolution. 2 Vols. in 1. 63 cts.

SOYER'S Modern Domestic Cookery. 12mo. Paper cover, 75 cts.; bd., $1.

SCOTT'S Lady of the Lake. 38 cents.

SCOTT'S Marmion. 16mo. 37 cts.

——— Lay of the Last Minstrel. 25 cents.

SELECT Italian Comedies. Translated. 12mo. 75 cts.

SPRAGUE'S History of the Florida War. Map and Plates. 8vo. $2 50.

SHAKSPEARE'S Dramatic Works and Life. 1 Vol., 8vo. $2.

SOUTHEY'S Life of Oliver Cromwell. 18mo. Cloth, 38 cts.

STEWART'S Stable Economy. Edited by A. B. Allen. 12mo. Illustrated. $1

SOUTHGATE (Bishop). Visit to the Syrian Church. 12mo. $1.

SQUIER'S Nicaragua; Its People, Antiquities, &c. Maps and Plates. 2 Vols., 8vo. $5.

STEVENS' Campaigns of the Rio Grande and Mexico. 8vo. Paper, 38 cts.

SWETT, Dr. Treatise on the Diseases of the Chest. 8vo. $3.

TAYLOR, Gen. Anecdote Book, Letters, &c. 8vo. 25 cts.

TUCKERMAN'S Artist Life. Biographical Sketches of American Painters. 12mo. Cloth, 75 cts.

TAYLOR'S Manual of Ancient and Modern History. Edited by Prof. Henry. 8vo. Cloth, $2 25; sheep, $2 50.

THOMSON on the Food of Animals and Man. Cloth, 50 cts.; paper, 38 cts.

TYSON, J. L. Diary of a Physician in California. 8vo. Paper, 25 cts.

WAYLAND'S Recollections of Real Life in England. 18mo. 31 cts.

WILLIAMS' Isthmus of Tehuantepec; Its Climate, Productions, &c. Maps and Plates. 2 Vols., 8vo. $3 50.

WOMAN'S Worth; or, Hints to Raise the Female Character. 18mo. 38 cts.

WARNER'S Rudimental Lessons in Music. 18mo. 50 cts.

WYNNE, J. Lives of Eminent Literary and Scientific Men of America. 12mo. Cloth, $1.

WORDSWORTH, W. The Prelude. An Autobiographical Poem. 12mo. Cloth, $1.

LAW BOOKS.

ANTHON'S Law Study; or, Guides to the Study of the Law. 8vo. $3.

HOLCOMBE'S Digest of the Decisions of the Supreme Court of the United States, from its commencement to the present time. Large 8vo. Law sheep, $6.

——— Supreme Court Leading Cases in Commercial Law. 8vo. $4.

——— Law of Debtor and Creditor in the United States and Canada. 8vo. $4.

SMITH'S Compendium of Mercantile Law. With large American additions by Holcombe and Gholson. 8vo. $4 50.

SCIENTIFIC WORKS.

APPLETON. Dictionary of Mechanics, Machines, Engine Work, and Engineering, containing over 4000 Illustrations, and nearly 2000 pages. Complete in 2 Vols., large 8vo. Strongly and neatly bound, $12.

APPLETON. Mechanics' Magazine and Engineers' Journal. Edited by Julius W. Adams, C. E. Published monthly, 25 cents per No., or $3 per annum. Vol. I. for 1851, in cloth, $3 50.

ARCHITECTURE AND BUILDING, Treatises on. By Hosking, Tredgood, and Young. Illustrated with 36 steel plates. 4to. $3 50.

ALLEN, Z. Philosophy of the Mechanics of Nature. Illus. 8vo. $3 50

ARNOT, D. H. Gothic Architecture, Applied to Modern Residences. 40 Plates. 1 Vol., 4to. $4.

ARTISAN CLUB. Treatise on the Steam Engine. Edited by J. Bourne. 33 Plates, and 349 Engravings on wood. 4to. $6.

BOURNE, JOHN. A Catechism of the Steam Engine. 16mo. 75 cts.

BYRNE, O. New Method of Calculating Logarithms. 12mo. $1.

BOUISSINGAULT, J. B. Rural Economy in its Relations with Chemistry, Physics, and Meteorology. 12mo. $1 25.

CULLUM, CAPT. On Military Bridges with India Rubber Pontoons, Illustrated. 8vo. $2.

DOWNING, A. I. Architecture of Country Houses. Including Designs for Cottages, Farm Houses, and Villas; with Remarks on Interiors, Furniture, and the best modes of Warming and Ventilating; with 320 Illustrations. 1 Vol., 8vo. $4.

——————— Architecture of Cottages and Farm Houses. Being the first part of his work on Country Houses, containing designs for Farmers, and those who desire to build cheap Houses. 8vo. $2.

GRIFFITHS, JOHN W. Treatise on Marine and Naval Architecture; or, Theory and Practice Blended in Ship-Building. 50 Plates. $10.

HALLECKS. Military Art and Science. 12mo. $1 50.

HAUPT, H. Theory of Bridge Construction. With Practical Illustrations. 8vo. $3.

HOBLYN, R. D. A Dictionary of Scientific Terms. 12mo. $1 50.

HODGE, P. R. On the Steam Engine. 48 large Plates, folio; and letter-press, 8vo. size. $8.

JEFFERS. Theory and Practice of Naval Gunnery. 8vo. Illus. $2 50.

KNAPEN, D. M. Mechanic's Assistant, adapted for the use of Carpenters, Lumbermen, and Artisans generally. 12mo. $1.

LAFEVER, M. Beauties of Modern Architecture. 48 Plates, large 8vo. $4.

LIEBIG, JUSTUS. Familiar Letters on Chemistry. 18mo. 25 cents.

OVERMAN, F. Metallurgy; embracing Elements of Mining Operations, Analyzation of Ores, &c. 8vo. Illustrated.

PARNELL, E. A. Chemistry Applied to the Arts and Manufactures. Illustrated. 8vo. Cloth, $1.

REYNOLDS, L. E. Treatise on Handrailing. Twenty Plates. 8vo. $2.

SYDNEY, J. C. Villa and Cottage Architecture. Comprising Residences actually built. Publishing in Nos., each No. containing 3 Plates, with Ground Plan, price 50 cents. (To be completed in 10 Nos.) 1 to 6 ready.

TEMPLETON, W. Mechanic, Millwright, and Engineers' Pocket Companion. With American Additions. 16mo. $1.

URE, DR. Dictionary of Arts, Manufactures, and Mines. New Edition, with Supplement. 8vo. Sheep, $5.

——— Supplement to do., separate. 8vo. Sheep, $1.

YOUMAN, E. L. Class-book of Chemistry. 12mo. 75 cents.

————— Chart of Chemistry, on Roller. $5.

ILLUSTRATED STANDARD POETS.

AMELIA'S Poems. Beautifully Illustrated by Robert W. Weir 8vo. Cloth, $2 50; gilt edges, $3; imperial mor., $3 50; morocco, $4.

BYRON'S Complete Poetical Works. Illustrated with elegant Steel Engravings and Portrait. 1 vol., 8vo., fine paper. Cloth, $3; cloth, gilt leaves, $4; morocco extra, $6.

Cheaper Edition, with Portrait and 4 Plates. Im. morocco, $3; with Portrait and Vignette only, sheep or cloth, $2 50.

HALLECK'S Complete Poetical Works. Beautifully Illustrated with fine Steel Engravings and a Portrait. New Edition. 8vo. Cloth, $2 50; cloth extra, gilt edges, $3; morocco extra, $5.

MOORE'S Complete Poetical Works. Illustrated with very fine Steel Engravings and a Portrait. 1 vol., 8vo., fine paper. Cloth, $3; cloth, gilt edges, $4; morocco, $6.

Cheaper Edition, with Portrait and 4 Plates. Im. morocco, $3; with Portrait and Vignette only, sheep or cloth, $2 50.

SOUTHEY'S Complete Poetical Works. With several beautiful Steel Engravings. 1 vol., 8vo., fine paper. Cloth, $3; gilt edges, $4 50; morocco, $6 50.

THE SACRED POETS OF ENGLAND AND AMERICA, for Three Centuries. Edited by Rufus W. Griswold. Illustrated with 12 Steel Engravings. 8vo. Cloth, $2 50; gilt edges, $3; morocco extra, $4 50.

Cabinet Editions, at greatly Reduced Prices.

BUTLER'S HUDIBRAS. With Notes by Nash. Illustrated with Portraits. 16mo. Cloth, $1; gilt edges, $1 50; moroc. extra, $2.

BURNS' Complete Poetical Works. With Life, Glossary, &c. 16mo. Cloth, illustrated, $1; gilt edges, $1 50; morocco extra, $2.

CAMPBELL'S Complete Poetical Works. Illustrated with Steel Engravings and a Portrait. 16mo. Cloth, $1; gilt edges, $1 50; morocco extra, $2.

COWPER'S Complete Poetical Works. With Life, &c. 2 vols. in 1. Cloth, $1; gilt, $1 50; morocco extra, $2.

DANTE'S Poems. Translated by Carey. Illustrated with a fine Portrait and 12 Engravings. 16mo. Cloth, $1; gilt edges, $1 50 morocco extra, $2.

HEMANS' Complete Poetical Works. Edited by her Sister 2 vols., 16mo. With 10 Steel Plates. Cloth, $2; gilt edges, $3; morocco extra, $4.

MILTON'S Complete Poetical Works. With Life, &c. 16mo. Cloth, illustrated, $1; gilt edges, $1 50; morocco extra, $2.

TASSO'S Jerusalem Delivered. Translated by Wiffen. Illustrated. 1 vol., 16mo. Uniform with "Dante." Cloth, $1; gilt edges, $1 50; morocco extra, $2.

SCOTT'S Poetical Works. With Life, &c. Cloth, 16mo., illustrated, $1; gilt, $1 50; morocco extra, $2.

RELIGIOUS.

ARNOLD'S Rugby School Sermons. 16mo. 50 cents.
ANTHON'S Catechism on the Homilies. 18mo. 6 cents.
———— Early Catechism for Young Children. 18mo. 6 cents.
A KEMPIS, Of the Imitation of Christ. 16mo. Complete Edition. 75 cts.
BURNETT'S History of the Reformation. Edited by Dr. Nares. 3 vols. $2 50.
———— On the Thirty-nine Articles. Edited by Page. 8vo. $2.
BRADLEY'S Family and Parish Sermons. Complete in 1 vol. $2.
CRUDEN'S Concordance to the New Testament. 12mo. 50 cents.
COTTER. The Romish Mass and Rubrics. Translated. 18mo. 38 cts.
COIT, Dr. Puritanism Reviewed. 12mo. $1.
EVANS' Rectory of Valehead. 16mo. 50 cents.
LIGHT IN THE DWELLING. (A Practical Family Commentary on the Four Gospels.) By the author of "Peep of Day." Edited by Dr. Tyng. Illustrated. 8vo. Cloth, $2; gilt edges, $2 50; im. morocco, $3 50; morocco, $4 50.
GRESLEY'S Portrait of an English Churchman. 50 cents.
———— Treatise on Preaching. 12mo. $1 25.
GRIFFIN, G. The Gospel its own Advocate. 12mo. $1.
HOOKER'S Complete Works. Edited by Keble. 2 vols. $4 50.
IVES' (Bishop) Sermons. 16mo. 50 cents.
JAMES' Happiness; its Nature and Sources.
JARVIS' Reply to Milner's End of Controversy. 12mo. 75 cents.
KINSGLEY'S Sacred Choir. 75 cents.
KIP'S Early Conflicts of Christianity. 12mo. 75 cents.
LYRA APOSTOLICA. 13mo. 50 cents.
MARSHALL'S Notes on Episcopacy. Edited by Wainwright. 12mo. $1.
MANNING on the Unity of the Church. 16mo. 75 cents.
MAURICE on the Kingdom of Christ. 8vo. $2 50.
MAGEE on Atonement and Sacrifice. 2 vols., 8vo. $5.
NEWMAN'S Sermons on Subjects of the Day. 12mo. $1.
———— Essay on Christian Doctrine. 8vo. Cloth, 75 cents.
OGILBY on Lay Baptism. 12mo. 50 cents.
PEARSON on the Creed. Edited by Dobson. Best Edition. 8vo. $2.
PULPIT CYCLOPÆDIA AND MINISTER'S COMPANION. 8vo. 600 pages. $2 50.
PSALTER (The), or Psalms of David. Pointed for Chanting. Edited by Dr. Muhlenberg. 12mo. Sheep, 50 cents; half cloth, 38 cents.
SEWELL. Readings for Every Day in Lent. 12mo. Cloth, 75 cents.
SOUTHARD. "The Mysteries of Godliness." 8vo. 75 cents.
SKETCHES AND SKELETONS OF 500 SERMONS. By the Author of "The Pulpit Cyclopædia." 8vo. $2 50.
SPENCER'S Christian Instructed. 16mo. $1.
SHERLOCK'S Practical Christian. 16mo. 75 cents.
SPINCKE'S Manual of Private Devotion. 16mo. 75 cents.
SUTTON'S Disce Vivere, Learn to Live. 16mo. 75 cents.
SWARTZ'S Letters to My Godchild. 32mo. Gilt edge, 38 cents.
TRENCH'S Notes on the Parables. 8vo. $1 75.
———— Notes on the Miracles of our Lord. 8vo. $1 75.
TAYLOR'S Holy Living and Dying. 12mo. $1.
———— Episcopacy Asserted and Maintained. 16mo.
WATSON'S Lecture on Confirmation. 18mo. Paper, 6 cents.
WILBERFORCE'S Manual for Communicants. 32mo. Gilt edges, 38 cts.
WILSON'S Lectures on Colossians. 12mo. 75 cents.
———— Sacra Privata. Complete Edition. 16mo. 75 cents.
———— Sacra Privata. 48mo. Cloth, 37 cents; roan, 50 cents.
WHISTON'S Constitution of the Holy Apostles, including the Canons. Translated by Dr. Chase. 8vo. $2 50.
WYATT's Christian Altar. New Edition. 32mo. Cloth, gilt edges, 38 cts.

COLLEGE AND SCHOOL TEXT-BOOKS.

Greek and Latin.

ARNOLD'S First and Second Latin Book and Practical Grammar. By Spencer. 12mo. 75 cents.

——— First Latin Book. By Harkness. 12mo. 75 cts.

——— Latin Prose Composition. 12mo. $1.

——— Cornelius Nepos. With Notes. 12mo. $1.

——— First Greek Book. New Edition, revised. 75 cts.

——— Greek Prose Composition. New Revised Edition. 12mo. 75 cents.

——— Second Greek Prose Composition. 12mo. 75 cts.

——— Greek Reading Book. Edited by Spencer. 12mo. $1 25.

BOISE'S Exercises in Greek Prose Composition. 12mo. 75 cts.

BEZA'S Latin Testament. 12mo. 62 cents.

CÆSAR'S Commentaries. Notes by Spencer. 12mo. $1.

CICERO De Officiis. Notes by Thatcher. 12mo. 90 cents.

——— Select Orations. Notes by Johnson. 12mo. $1.

KENDRICK'S Greek Ollendorff. 12mo. $1.

HORACE. With Notes, &c. By Lincoln. 12mo. $1 25.

KUHNER'S Elementary Greek Grammar. By Edwards and Taylor. New improved Edition. 12mo. (In press.)

LIVY. With Notes, &c. By Lincoln. 12mo. Map. $1.

TACITUS' Histories. Notes by Tyler. 12mo. $1.

——— Germania and Agricola. Notes by Tyler. 12mo. 62 cents.

XENOPHON'S Memorabilia. Notes by Robbins. New Revised Edition. 18mo. (In press.)

Hebrew.

GESENIUS' Hebrew Grammar. Edited by Rödiger. Translated from the best German Edition, by Conant. 8vo $2.

www.ingramcontent.com/pod-product-compliance
Lightning Source LLC
LaVergne TN
LVHW020056110826
845151LV00005B/1495

* 9 7 8 1 4 2 5 5 2 2 5 2 0 *